ADVANCE F

"Scott's is a story at once great storyteller because we are invited to reflect how his story is our story, and even a part of the sacred story of God's dance with each of us. I found myself pausing often to reflect on my own journey as Scott's honesty startled me into nostalgia. It is also a story of hope. A good story speaks for people as much as to people and *Open* invites us to do just that as we hear our story in Scott Jones'. This opened my heart anew in some very important ways, and hopefully it will do the same for you."

—Michael Piazza
*Founding pastor of Cathedral of Hope
and author of* Gay by God

"This is a touching memoir—a coming out story in the best sense of the genre. Coming out is never simply a one-time grand confessional but it's about the continual work of discerning and living our truths in community. While bravery is certainly required to come out, perhaps even more central is curiosity about ourselves and the people who inhabit our lives. Such curiosity also makes for great storytelling as it does in Scott's memoir. Scott has provided us with a glimpse into the experience of living openly as a Southern gay Christian minister. This is an important book that I hope is widely read."

—Sharon Groves
*Vice President for Partner Engagement at Auburn
Seminary and former Director of the Religion and
Faith Program at the Human Rights Campaign*

"Scott movingly and eloquently describes his struggle to reconcile his sexuality with his deep Christian spirituality."

—Terence Hawkins
*Founding director of the Yale Writer's Conference
and author of* American Neolithic

"Scott Jones has given us an important first-person account of queer Christian life in Middle America. A narrative companion to the "rural turn" in LGBTQ scholarship, *Open* explores the heartache and triumphs of growing up and coming out in Texas and Oklahoma. This is a tale of the personal and political courage it takes to face moral entrepreneurs who equate homosexuality with terrorism and peddle other anti-gay snake oil. Jones's story inspires!"

—Carol Mason
Author of Oklahomo: Lessons in Unqueering America

"*Open* is hard to put down, Scott Jones is unflinching in his candidness about his coming out journey as a man of faith. As you read his story you get no respite from feeling deeply. I cried, I laughed, I cheered him on for his bravery. It was an eye-opening narrative, even for a queer woman of color like myself."

—Ruth Marimo
Author of OUTsider: Crossing Borders.
Breaking Rules. Gaining Pride

"Scott is honest and expansive in his treatment of events, and his writing is clear, poignant, open, and often funny. Scott's story is one that will give hope to young and old people caught in the morass of anti-LGBTQ traditions."

—Greg Horton
Freelance writer and adjunct professor

Open

A Memoir of Faith, Family,
and Sexuality in the Heartland

E. SCOTT JONES

Open: A Memoir Of Faith, Family,
And Sexuality in the Heartland

Copyright © 2018 by E. Scott Jones

ISBN 9781943988105

Edited by Rebecca Rutledge and Charles Martin
Cover and layout design by April Marciszewski

Dedicated to my grandparents:

Christine & Herbert Jones
Eleanor & Willard Nixon

ACKNOWLEDGMENTS

When I finally came out publicly in 2005, I decided to write about my journey on my personal blog. After years of secrecy, the open sharing of my story was scary. Soon after the initial rush, I began to ponder if this story of coming out while a Baptist youth minister in Texas could be developed into a memoir.

In 2009 I published an essay "On Being an Openly Gay Minister in a Red State" in Prism: A Theological Forum for the United Church of Christ, Volume 23, Number 2, Fall 2009. The essay told some of the story related here in chapter 24, "Sally Kern."

Over the years, as the story was still unfolding, I was also writing about it. But the memoir languished.

In 2014 I saw an advertisement in *The New Yorker* for that summer's Yale Writer's Conference. A Lily grant for pastoral excellence was available to me through the Nebraska Conference of the United Church of Christ. So I applied to Yale with an excerpt from this memoir and was thrilled when I was accepted. I used the grant money to underwrite the conference fees.

Attending that conference I had two big questions—was this a worthy project and did I have the talent and ability to keep working on it? My faculty and colleagues answered those questions in the affirmative.

So I devoted the next year to completing a first full draft and returned to the Yale Writer's Conference in 2015 as part of a memoir intensive. The last two years have been spent in revisions and editing.

I want to thank First Central Congregational United Church

of Christ in Omaha, Nebraska for giving me opportunities to explore my writing and time off to work on this book.

Thanks are due to the *Oklahoma Gazette* and *Hard News Online* for opportunities to write as a columnist in the first decade of this century. My editors Rob Collins, Jon Horinek, and Michael Bratcher improved my writing.

Thank you to the faculty of the Yale Writer's Conference, including founding director Terrence Hawkins, Colleen Kinder, Robin Hemley, Lisa Page, and Eileen Pollack for their guidance, criticisms, and encouragement.

Thank you to Cheryl Strayed and Rick Moody for their master classes. A special thanks to Rick Moody who said to me over lunch following that class, "You have what it takes. Good luck."

The other students in my workshops contributed ideas and friendship that have helped me as a writer. I especially want to thank Christie Platt, Nancy Gray, Shawn Crawford, and Christopher Gilson. In Chris I found my most effective reader. Whenever I was puzzling over how to improve a section of the book, Chris usually suggested the solution.

I thank Marty Peercy for his years of friendship and his encouragement of my writing. Marty doesn't appear as a character in the final draft of this memoir, but he has helped to shape both it and my personal story.

In the spring of 2016 Charles Martin visited Omaha, and we discussed this book. We have known each other since college and wrote for the *Oklahoma Gazette* at the same time (in fact, Charles got me that gig). I am grateful that he chose to publish it through Literati Press. Thank you for believing in the importance of this story.

Rebecca Rutledge edited the book and her suggestions greatly improved it. Thank you for your care.

Finally, this book wouldn't exist if my husband Michael Cich-Jones hadn't supported the effort. Shortly after I completed the first full draft our son Sebastian was born, and six weeks later I left for eleven days to attend the Yale Writer's Conference. When I returned Michael said, "Never again."

But he has insisted on celebrating each milestone as I moved to completion.

Peace,

Scott Jones
Omaha, Nebraska
July 21, 2017

A NOTE ON NAMES

Some of the names in this book are changed, and some are not.

I did not change the names of anyone who is deceased.

I did not change the names of public figures, including fellow clergy persons.

Some people expressly said I could use their names, so I did.

I changed the names of congregants in the churches I have served. Some who read this book thought I should share more stories about my ministry, but I have mostly avoided that out of respect for the relationship between pastor and congregation.

I changed the names of most of the people I have dated or had sex with in the story, with a few notable exceptions.

And I changed the names of most of my living family members.

The ethics of writing about family and friends is central to memoir. In writing about them I have tried to be honest and respectful. Changing names was suggested by some of my teachers as a way of offering family members further respect.

1

Driving on Christmas Morning

Driving on Christmas morning is unlike driving any other day of the year. Because the cars are few, a quiet stillness hovers over the road. And those who are out driving seem determined to get where they are headed, often with their backseats crammed with luggage, gifts, and kids. The radio is filled with bad Christmas music, even on the stations that haven't been playing it round the clock since Halloween. So, driving on Christmas morning, you've got plenty of time to think.

I was headed home to Miami, Oklahoma, to my grandpa's house, and I didn't want to be the one everyone was waiting on. I remembered all those times my family sat around waiting for someone who was late to show up and how everyone complained and criticized. The day before, I had packed all my luggage in the car so I could awaken early on Christmas morning and simply get on the open road.

I had also cleaned and readied my house because when I returned from the holiday with family, John was coming to visit. I was going to tell him I wanted to explore a relationship with him. And I'd never been in a relationship with a man before.

Regardless of what my conservative family of Oklahoma Baptists might think about that, on this Christmas morning, I was determined to be neither the cause of delay nor the object of their complaints.

Back in October, Sarah's phone call had caught me at home one evening while I was lying on the couch watching *Angel*.

"John's coming to town the weekend of Halloween," she'd said. "You should come over and hang out with us."

I had moved to Dallas the previous winter to become the Associate Pastor for Youth and Education at Royal Lane Baptist Church. Sarah and her husband, Lucas, both friends of mine from college, moved there a few months later.

"After all," Sarah had continued, "John has had a crush on you for over two years."

I smiled and shook my head. "Yes, I know. You've told me that before. Like every time he comes up in conversation."

"And as I've said before, you would be perfect for each other."

"Except," I said—and here Sarah and I spoke in unison—"the only problem is that I am straight."

Her tone of voice conveyed that she had said 'straight' with quote marks.

I added, "That really is a problem, you know?"

"I know. Except that in every other way I think you are perfect for each other. You both read a lot, you both grew up in church, and you are both obsessed with *Buffy*."

"I am watching *Angel* right now," I said.

"See?"

We both laughed. "Okay," I said. "I'll come over. I've got a youth group party for church that night, but I'll come over after that. I'll probably be in costume, but maybe I'll bring something to change into. Even if I am straight, I do enjoy talking with John."

"Then it's settled," she said with glee. "See you Saturday."

Sarah and I had met through mutual friends in the late Nineties, when I was in graduate school pursuing my PhD in philosophy at the University of Oklahoma. I was living in Shawnee, the small town where I'd done my undergraduate schooling at Oklahoma Baptist University. Many of my friends in those years were students who enjoyed coming over to my house for weekend parties. I had the nice deck and the hot tub. Plus, I kept my house clean.

Sarah lived in the apartment building around the corner. One evening I went to hang out with her and met John, her older brother.

He was slightly taller than me and just a couple of years younger. He had light brown hair and a thin goatee. Wire-rimmed glasses didn't hide his brown eyes. John and I talked about *Buffy*, the *Harry Potter* books, and how he thought *The Waste Land* was T. S. Eliot's prank on the literary world. I invited him to walk around the corner to see my house.

I was simply not dressed to impress. I was in a Star Trek T-shirt, shorts that he later said he thought were too short (though he admitted that's what folks were wearing at the time), and a tired pair of sandals.

I gave him the grand tour of my thousand-square-foot home, and then we settled into the living room. The conversation continued until he said goodbye and I saw him to the door.

Had John made a move, the evening would have ended differently.

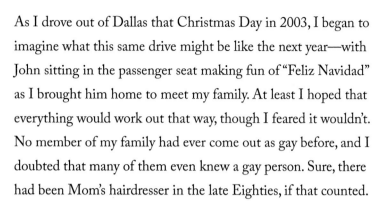

As I drove out of Dallas that Christmas Day in 2003, I began to imagine what this same drive might be like the next year—with John sitting in the passenger seat making fun of "Feliz Navidad" as I brought him home to meet my family. At least I hoped that everything would work out that way, though I feared it wouldn't. No member of my family had ever come out as gay before, and I doubted that many of them even knew a gay person. Sure, there had been Mom's hairdresser in the late Eighties, if that counted.

Plus, there was that other issue. I was a Baptist minister. Working with teenagers. In Texas.

Back in first grade, Mrs. Pittman gave us an assignment to draw a picture of what we wanted to be when we grew up. I sketched out mere stick figures with no aesthetic merit. In the drawing, I am standing at a pulpit, preaching. Just below and to the left of the pulpit is a row of pews. And on the first pew I drew my mother, sitting and listening with a smile on her face.

Being a minister is what I've always wanted; it's a core truth of who I am. But it's not the only one. Would exploring my sexuality force me out of the ministry? If so, who was I if I wasn't a minister?

Since seeing John again in October, I had been wrestling with all these questions and felt that finally I had made a choice to live with courage and integrity by claiming my full, authentic identity.

Crossing the border into southeastern Oklahoma, I began to wonder about something else—my own hopes for a family. I'd always dreamed of being an old man, sitting around the

Thanksgiving table with my children and grandchildren. Could I have children, grandchildren, and a family if I came out? Would this decision make that dream an impossibility, too?

U.S. Highway 69 passes over Lake Eufaula. The water is a muddy red color. The lake is human-made and hopelessly stained by the soil below it.

I put the worries out of my mind and began to fantasize. John and I would get married. Maybe our wedding would be at the home of church members where I had gone for a day of private retreat back in November in order to contemplate the conflict between these two callings—to sexual authenticity and Christian ministry.

I pictured a sunny day at the two-story, white-columned house beside a clear lake. All of our friends and family would be gathered around us. My many friends in ministry would be there expressing their friendship to me and their solidarity on the issue of gay marriage. After our kiss, the audience would cheer and applaud, and we'd celebrate with barbecue on the lawn as the sunset glistened over the water.

And we would have children. Somehow. Adoption, possibly. But maybe we could get our sisters to donate eggs, and we could create embryos that, in the only path open to us, would be genetically related to us both. Yes, I was sure that day. This life was possible.

Soon I saw the sign indicating my exit. The time had passed more quickly than I'd anticipated; I'd been captivated by my fantasies. As I exited the turnpike for my hometown, I was hopeful that everything would work out—family, ministry, love, and my true self.

2

"It was like The Beverly Hillbillies."

I consider my hometown, Miami, to be a typical American small town, except for one detail. The name is pronounced "My-am-uh." As I always say, "That's spelled the same as the city in Florida, but pronounced correctly."

We are located in the northeastern corner of Oklahoma with rolling pastures of soybeans that turn a deep, rich green in late spring. The landscape and agricultural life are very Midwestern, but the people identify as Southerners. Elders informed us children that in their lifetimes, a sign was posted at the city limits warning black people (though a different word was used) to be out of town by sundown. Even in my childhood, the community was predominantly white. There were only two African-American students in school with me.

The largest B. F. Goodrich tire factory in the United States dominated the northwestern edge of town. The plant was the source of our middle-class economy, for a young man could graduate high school and the next week get a good union job at the plant. By his thirties he might be doing well enough to own a boat and a lake cabin. The plant was an incredible economic engine, and we were not the poor, struggling, rural small town that is much more common in America these days. The children of plant workers usually ended up going off to college. Generations of those kids returned to become the town's professional class—doctors, lawyers, pharmacists, bankers, and professors.

Main Street was a thriving business district with Woolworth's, Sears, J. C. Penney, Montgomery Ward, and local department stores. The landmark of Main Street was the Coleman Theatre Beautiful, a grand cinema built in 1929 with an elaborate Spanish Revival exterior and a rich Louis XIV interior. The big red-and-white marquee with bright flashing lights invited generations of Miamians to theatrical productions and films. Grandma Jones enjoyed telling the story of her first date in a car, when the young man picked her up in a Model T and drove her from the farm to Miami to see a film at the Coleman. The car ride was a fun adventure, she told me, and the bright lights dazzled her.

At its peak, Miami's population was only 15 thousand. We were a wonderful example of the golden age of small-town America.

The factory closed in 1986. The downtown department stores disappeared not long after. Families uprooted themselves and departed for towns where they could find jobs. And fewer and fewer kids who went away returned.

My grandfather's house wasn't far from the exit off Interstate 44, the Will Rogers Turnpike. "Pappoo" is the name I had given him when I was a small child, and the nickname had stuck all those decades. Like me, Pappoo was born in Miami. His family survived the Great Depression eating beans three times a day.

Pappoo's father was an extroverted, jovial man. "He smiled and laughed often," Mom would say when I asked about her family. "His belly jiggled like Santa Claus." Then she would sigh and add, "I loved my grandfather very much."

Her grandmother was a different story. "She was a bitter woman," Mom told me. "She never said 'I love you.' She never baked me cookies or pies. She never hugged me or held me or encouraged me." And then Mom would sigh in a different way.

My great-grandmother had been one of nineteen children raised by a family with money and land. The family's monument in the local Grand Army of the Republic cemetery is a massive black granite monolith etched with their name, "England." When her parents died, her brothers inherited land, but she and her sisters received only $100 each. And $100 didn't last long when the Depression came. My mother always assumed her grandmother's bitterness resulted from the swift decline in her fortunes from comfort and wealth to a struggling life of poverty.

At family gatherings I would ask my great-aunts and great-uncles about their experiences. Pappoo's sister Lavenia enjoyed storytelling. "When the Depression came, our parents loaded up the six of us kids and all our belongings on the Model T," she told me once. "It was like *The Grapes of Wrath* or *The Beverly Hillbillies*," she said, laughing. "We traveled the country looking for work. Once, when we were in Colorado, the car couldn't make it up the hills and mountains loaded down with so many people and things, so we all had to get out and walk as the car sputtered its way to the top."

Pappoo, Mom, my sister Erin, and I drove up to Springfield, Missouri one day to visit my Aunt Karen.

On the way, Pappoo wanted to stop in Bois D'Arc (pronounced Bo-dark) to locate one of the homes they had all lived in during those Depression-era wanderings. The house was long gone, but we found the spot, just an empty field surrounded by woods. Standing there, his delight showed as he told us childhood stories.

My favorite one of those stories—and I think it was Pappoo's as well—was of one night when all the kids were crowded in the upstairs loft sleeping abreast of one another. Uncle George, one of Pappoo's older brothers, got diarrhea and couldn't get out of the upstairs and outside to the outhouse fast enough, so he just stuck his ass out the window and did his business down the side of the house.

Pappoo told us other idyllic stories from his childhood, of skinny dipping in the Neosho River or following the ice wagon on a hot summer day to pick up and eat the chunks that fell.

He was the first in his family to complete high school. He met my grandmother shortly before enlisting in the Army for service in the Second World War. He saw action in North Africa and was part of the Allied invasion of Italy. Initial reports were that he died during the landing at Anzio. But he was only wounded, though quite severely. He spent six months at a hospital in Naples and even longer convalescing back in the United States. Surgeons were unable to remove all the shrapnel, because a few chunks were quite close to his spine. He lived the rest of his life with the possibility that the shrapnel could shift, damage his spinal cord, and paralyze him.

Pappoo received the Purple Heart. But he never spoke about his honor. He found it unseemly when other veterans began acquiring license plates for their cars that indicated they were Purple Heart recipients.

With his GI Bill, Pappoo pursued an education and began a career, spending most of his adult life in the Postal Service and rising to become a postmaster, a distinguished career in small-town America.

Pappoo came to his faith as a young adult, not having been raised in a churchgoing family. After his profession of faith, he evangelized the rest of his family, who then became devoted Christians. For many decades he served as the fourth-grade Sunday school teacher at church. He often chaired the Properties Committee and was ordained as a Deacon, which in those days was the deeply respected council of prominent men who determined the business of the congregation. I grew up in the First Baptist Church where he was a leader.

On Christmas morning, I arrived at Pappoo's house a little earlier than I had anticipated. All the better, I thought. No one would be able to complain that I was the cause of delay. I took a deep breath as I pulled up across the street from his house. "Here goes," I said to myself. Suddenly, the doubts and fears I had struggled with for months came flooding back.

"Merry Christmas, Scotty," Pappoo called from the front porch with a big smile, his white hair perfectly combed. "Do you need help?" He came out to the street to assist me with my presents and luggage. "How was the drive?"

"Not bad. It flew by. Not much traffic, of course."

"How long did it take?" he asked, reaching to take a bag.

"About five and a half hours, I think."

My Mom's younger sister Karen met us in the entryway with a glass of pop in her hand. "We didn't expect you for a few more hours."

"Well, I said I'd be here by noon," I said with a puzzled look on my face. Pappoo and I began carrying my gifts into the living room to place under the tree.

"I guess we all thought it would take you longer than that. Most of the other folks aren't here yet. We won't be eating for a while," she said and took a sip of her pop.

"I'm starving," I said. "You can imagine there isn't much breakfast to find on the road on Christmas morning. I thought we were eating at noon; that's why I left so early and rushed here." I was more than a little put out. Then I asked, "Is there anything to eat?"

"Well, I guess we didn't understand you'd be here so soon," my aunt said. She led me into the kitchen and she handed me a bag of potato chips.

"I thought I was pretty clear in my e-mail," I said with some exasperation. I was thinking, *Didn't anyone listen to me?* I took the chips and looked around for something more substantial to eat.

Karen shrugged. "Oh, well," she said. "Have a snack and just wait on everyone else."

I long for the Christmas traditions of my childhood. On Christmas Eve mornings we would pack the car full of gifts and drive to the farm where Grandpa and Grandma Jones lived. They owned eighty acres a few miles outside of Miami in an old hamlet called Narcissa. Once there had been a school-house and a handful of businesses there, but by my childhood only a gas station and the Baptist church remained. U.S. 69 passed through without even a four-way stop. At least the speed limit slowed to 45 for a few blocks.

At the top of a tall hill in the center of the farm, there was a rock-covered hole that Grandma Jones told us was an old Indian well. A creek cut through the property and fed two ponds. Just beyond the yard was an old pear tree. The giant goldfish swimming in one of the ponds were descended from a few normal-sized ones that my Dad had dumped in the water when he was a kid. Or so I'd been told.

As a child I would wander those fields and climb the hill, play in the barns and in the hay shed, and swing on the tire hanging from the catalpa tree outside the kitchen window. On the Fourth of July, we would spend the day on the farm. The women cooked while the men sat under that tree and turned the ice cream freezer by hand. At dark, as the adults sat in the white Adirondack chairs, we'd shoot off our small fireworks out by the old chicken house and watch the bigger shows of neighboring towns along the horizon.

At Christmas, the cold weather prevented outside adven-tures, so we warmed ourselves by the furnace and indulged in homemade candies. Aunt Mae's divinity was my favorite. The white fluff would melt in my mouth, and I'd crunch the nuts. My sister Erin and I were always able to convince Grandma Jones to let us open our presents before the family ate lunch.

Grandma Jones liked to grab us and give us sloppy kisses on the cheek. She wore loose-fitting housedresses and spent most days in the kitchen. She made the most deliciously juicy hamburgers; to this day I've never eaten one as good as hers. She would fill her cast-iron skillet with Crisco and fry them on the stove. Then, after the burgers were good and cooked, she'd lay the buns down into the skillet to brown them, ladling grease over them with a spoon, making sure the fat soaked in. Those burgers tasted amazing, but my arteries are probably glad I haven't had one in decades.

We didn't eat hamburgers at Christmas, of course. Grandma and my aunts would have spent all morning, and probably a few days before, preparing a giant spread including turkey, ham, mashed potatoes, green beans, corn, peas, and chicken and noodles—my favorite, and one of Grandma's specialties.

Grandpa Jones was an old cowboy who loved to laugh and crack jokes. He also delighted in tickling his grandkids, but when he did, he dug into our ribs and armpits so hard it hurt. When we were really little, he'd take us on drives through the fields to see the cows. He invited me along once as the young steers were collected and delivered to the slaughterhouse. Grandpa would put his big hat on my little head and let me pretend to be a rancher right along with him.

After Christmas lunch at the Jones's , we'd pack up our gifts and head into town for dinner at Pappoo's and Mammoo's— the Nixons, my Mom's parents. For much of my childhood, they lived near Main Street in Miami in a big, white, two-story house. When we stayed with them we'd walk down to Main Street and browse the stores, spend time at the public library, or pick out some ceramics to paint at the ceramics store.

When you spent the night at their house, you awakened in

the morning not to some noisy alarm, nor to sunlight streaming through curtains or the sound of birds singing in the trees,
but to the smell of frying bacon wafting up from the kitchen
where Mammoo was fixing breakfast. No better way exists to
awaken in the morning.

Besides the home in town, the Nixons also owned a cabin on
Grand Lake in Grove, only about a half hour south of Miami.
Because of them I grew up fishing, boating, and trying to learn
to water ski, which I never accomplished. They'd throw big fam-
ily barbecues and fish fries and invite all their siblings and all my
Mom's cousins, and maybe forty or fifty people would be there.

But Christmas was only about a dozen of us. We never could
convince Mammoo to let us open presents first. At her house,
you always ate first, and the kids were relegated to the small
table in the kitchen.

Mammoo wore her brown hair in a tall beehive hairdo. She
loved to read and craft and fish. She was very particular; no
food or drinks in the living room. Blue was her favorite color.
Even her trash bags were blue.

After Christmas Eve dinner and the exchange of presents,
we would head back to our house where we read the Christmas
story, celebrated Jesus' birthday with a birthday cake, and then
opened our gifts for each other, just Mom, Dad, Erin, and
myself. Then it was off to bed so we could get up early in the
morning to see what Santa delivered on Christmas Day.

In January of 1988, after a lifetime of smoking, Grandpa
Jones died of lung cancer. Mammoo died of complications
from kidney stones just three months later. Many of our family
traditions changed that year. We now had one grandparent

who was a widow with declining health who required more care from us. The other grandparent was a widower who soon began dating, which was not something any of us were prepared to deal with. I had grown up with all these wonderful, idyllic experiences of family that suddenly came to an end; that year death felt like a constant presence in our lives.

So for spring break in March of 1990, it made sense that we decided to visit family. We went to Springfield, Missouri and stayed at Aunt Karen's house. One night some of us went to a basketball game at Southwest Missouri State University. As we waited for my uncle to get the tickets, my dad said to me, "I'm feeling a little stuffy in here; it's too crowded. Why don't we go back outside and get some fresh air?" The entrance to the gymnasium was packed with people.

We were separated as we exited, pushing against the flow of the crowd. Dad headed toward a retaining wall to sit down. As I was making my way toward him, he crumpled to the ground.

"Dad! Help!"

A sudden rush of activity surrounded us. Some people bent over him to see if he was okay. Others ran to call an ambulance. A stranger asked if he could do anything to help, and I described my uncle. The man went looking for him in the crowded ticket lines inside.

Dad sat up and leaned against the wall. "That's embarrassing," he said. "I just got a little stuffy with all the people around. I think I'm okay now." He grinned at me. He had this particular grin—sly, mischievous, and charming—where the right side of his mouth turned up more than the left.

He refused to go to the hospital when the ambulance arrived.

He insisted that he was feeling better. "I had a bout of heartburn on Wednesday, maybe this is related," he said. No encouragement from the EMTs or my uncle could change his mind. He told me that if he wasn't feeling better by tomorrow, we'd head back to Miami. "How about that?"

Who was I at sixteen to argue with my dad? So we decided to skip the game and go back to my aunt and uncle's. And I trusted him that everything would be okay.

My dad was born to a poor, neglectful, and abusive family outside Haskell, a town in the river land of eastern Oklahoma. His name at birth was Leonard Green and he was nicknamed "Tubby" because he was such a plump baby. He was spared the physical and sexual abuse experienced by his older sisters. He was a toddler when the state took them all away.

When he was four, my dad was brought down the stairs of the state orphanage to meet Herbert and Christine Jones. Knowing how loving and affectionate my grandmother was, I can only imagine how she must have scooped him up in her lap.

Dad grew up on the farm outside Miami, raised by two parents who had wanted a child for so long but had been unable to have one of their own. Even when he was an adult, Grandma would come up to him and stroke his arm and kiss his cheek. He didn't care for it, but you could tell from the look in her eyes that even all those years later Grandma was so grateful that this child had come into her life.

After a tour of duty in the Navy and a few years as a hospital administrator, Dad spent most of his career as an educator, first teaching middle school social studies and then working as a high school principal. He enjoyed fishing, hunting, and also reading a good book. He was as likely to take our family biking as he was to lead us in an educational game memorizing the presidents of the United States. He also enjoyed telling corny jokes.

That night after he collapsed at the basketball game, I was awakened at about three a.m. by my mother screaming. I rushed into Aunt Karen's guest bedroom. Mom stood over where Dad lay on the bed. His breaths were rapid hisses through a clenched jaw. His eyes did not move. He was not responsive.

Then he stopped breathing.

I had never been trained in CPR, but I'd seen enough television, so I beat his chest until he started breathing again. Soon, a neighbor who knew CPR arrived. "Pull him off the bed onto the floor," he ordered. He began to perform proper CPR. I held Dad's head in my hands as this stranger went to work.

Dad's breathing became shallower. The rate slowed. Beating on his chest didn't work a second time.

I wiped my father's brow with a wet cloth as he breathed his last breaths. I held him as he died. He was only forty-one. His first and only heart attack. I was sixteen.

Obviously, holidays were never the same again. No one hung around for hours playing games after presents were opened. No one spent days preparing candies and cooking meals. We gathered for a quick and easy lunch, caught up with each other, opened presents, and soon departed.

That Christmas at Pappoo's, after my long drive from Dallas, I was more energetic than usual, laughing at everyone's jokes, telling stories, and making sarcastic asides to my sister and cousin. Yet as everything began to wind down, I sat in the corner of the living room, watching my family go through their routines, and wondering what would happen to our relationships now as my life changed.

3

"Seems like the Bible is pretty clear to me."

The day after Christmas, I stayed on at Pappoo's after the rest of the family had departed. I wanted to spend more time with him, just in case things went bad in the next year.

When I was a kid, he would take me along to meetings at the church, where the elderly men would make important decisions. I delighted in discussing the Bible and church with him. As he moved with dignity and solemnity in the rituals of the Lord's Supper or as he prayed eloquently (better than the other Deacons), I watched him with focused attention.

Pappoo taught me how to fish. How to bait my hook and tie the line. How to hold the line gently in my right hand, tugging ever so slightly to entice the fish to swallow the bait. How to pull back sharply when you felt the fish had swallowed, to ensure the hook set. And then how to reel the line in carefully so as not to lose the catch.

In my teen years, he employed me in the summers to assist with yardwork and home remodeling, teaching me how to tape and mud, the proper way to paint, and to clean your tools when finished.

When I was ordained in 1997, the honor fell to my grandfather to be the first person to lay hands upon me and bless me.
I admired him and wanted to be like him for I sensed in him a
grace—a gentleness and kindness—that I didn't sense in a lot
of people.

But over time, he changed. Whereas he had once written a
letter to the editor of our local paper defending the rights of
others to burn the American flag because as a World War II
veteran he had fought defending those rights, he now listened
to Rush Limbaugh and watched Fox News and a bunch of
fundamentalist TV preachers. He had become religiously and
politically conservative. He had taken to giving waitresses
religious tracts.

The culture of the heartland was shifting. Oklahoma
had pretty much been a one-party Democratic state in my
childhood. In our county, every election was determined in
the Democratic primary. The only Republicans were liberal
Episcopalians. That shifted in the 1990s, reflecting regional
trends. Baptists, once solid Democrats, became Republicans.
People who had been yellow dog Democrats since the New
Deal were suddenly spouting right-wing ideas.

A more thorough historical analysis is necessary to understand these shifts, but my personal opinion is that they were
motivated by fear and disgust. The world into which these people had been born, the world they'd grown up in, was changing.
The great cultural movements of the 1960s and 1970s, which
were distant from much of the heartland, were finally having
an effect in the 1980s and 1990s. The election of Bill Clinton,
draft dodger and adulterer, repulsed people like Pappoo.

Some might think that while growing up at the First Baptist Church of Miami, Oklahoma, I often heard denunciations of homosexuality. That was not the case. The topic never came up. If someone had dared to raise the issue, of course the teaching would have been that homosexuality was a sin, but homosexuality never entered into our horizons as a topic that required our attention.

Two women in town lived together and most people knew they were a couple, but they made no public issue of that fact, so no one else did either. My mother would describe a few men as "light in the loafers," but she demonstrated pity towards their condition, not scorn. People gossiped about a lawyer who supposedly cross-dressed when out of town, but no one would have spoken openly about gender issues. If he didn't cross-dress around us, we could ignore the gossip. Plus, we were taught that gossiping was a sin. To act upon the gossip would have revealed one's own moral corruption.

The day after Christmas I was sitting on the couch with Pappoo and Sue, my step-grandmother, watching Bill Moyers on PBS. Sue wasn't paying attention to the program. Instead, she was trying to carry on a conversation with me. I was half engaged with her and half trying to listen to the TV, because Moyers was interviewing the Rev. Dr. James Forbes, then the Senior Minister at Riverside Church in New York City. At one point the interview turned to the topic of Riverside Church's inclusion of LGBT persons.

Pappoo, who had difficulty hearing, spoke up. "Are they talking about the gays?"

Without looking at him, I answered, "Yes." Sue kept talking, but Pappoo was focused on the interview.

"Are they saying they welcome them in that church?"

I wasn't prepared to have this conversation. "Yes, that is what they are saying." I kept my head turned toward the television, watching Pappoo out of the corner of my eye.

He asked earnestly but sharply, "Well, how could they do that?"

"Because they don't believe it's a sin. There are not only churches but entire denominations who don't believe the Bible is against homosexuality," I answered.

He shook his head and looked directly at me. "I just don't understand it. Seems like the Bible is pretty clear to me."

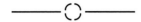

The Bible was clear to me as well, but I happened to agree with Rev. Forbes and the Riverside Church that Christians should welcome and include LGBT people. I struggled not with the theological question of whether it was okay to be gay and be a Christian but whether I had the courage and integrity to risk my home, my family, and my ministry in order to claim my full, authentic identity.

I had long before abandoned the conservative religious views I'd grown up with. My college education in biblical interpretation had taught me a lot about historical and cultural context. Plus, during college and grad school, a number of my close friends came out. I arrived at a theology of inclusion without the long personal struggle of so many gay evangelicals. Even at Oklahoma Baptist University, I publicly opposed the school's anti-gay policy. My letters on the topic were published in the campus newspaper, and I even wrote to the president of the university expressing my position.

The Baptists I had grown up with were definitely conservative Southerners, but they weren't, generally, biblical literalists and fundamentalists. We weren't the Jerry Falwell types (he wasn't even a Southern Baptist at that time, viewing us as too liberal). Many of the people I knew held to historic Baptist principles that included the separation of church and state, the freedom of the individual person to interpret the Bible for themselves, and the freedom of the local church to make its own decisions. Yes, these were principles that Baptists historically stood for and had, at times in the past, died for.

In 1979, a movement began that is described either as the "conservative resurgence" or the "fundamentalist takeover," depending on which side you were on. In a period when the newly developing religious right was gaining prominence in American politics, they were also gaining power in the denomination of my birth, shifting its approach on a wide variety of issues. People forget that the Southern Baptist Convention filed a brief in support of a woman's freedom to choose in the case of *Roe v. Wade*.

But what ensued in the 1980s was a fierce battle over the interpretation of the Bible and the role of women in the church. As more progressive and moderate congregations ordained women, they were often expelled from their local associations or state conventions. Many times these were historically prominent churches. All of the SBC's seminaries became battlefields and many professors and even seminary presidents were fired by boards that became increasingly more conservative. Contrary to myths of historic progress, the fundamentalist takeover that failed in the 1920s was successful in the 1980s.

As educators, my parents were deeply troubled by the firings at institutions of higher learning, even if they remained theologically conservative themselves. Most individual congregations and most individual church folk hated all the political fighting and simply stayed away from national and state meetings.

By 1990, every member of every board and commission had been appointed by the fundamentalists. They had completed their takeover. Whereas in prior decades denominational leaders had made a conscientious effort to keep a balance between moderate and conservative appointments (with the occasional progressive), now one side of the denomination held all the leadership posts.

As a result, the Cooperative Baptist Fellowship was formed in 1990. A group of moderates decided to start doing a new thing and give up trying to battle for leadership and control of the SBC. The simplest way to characterize the CBF is as "Jimmy Carter Baptists."

All of this change was fermenting while I was in college. Some of my classmates came from the most liberal churches in the SBC, so I learned from them different ways of being a Baptist than I'd learned from my small-town, conservative upbringing. My own views on a number of issues developed over these years as a result of my higher education. I rejected creationism, came to support the ordination of women, was deeply concerned about the environment, and changed my views on homosexuality.

Pappoo had never been sure of what to make of me after I went away to the state's Baptist college as a conservative and graduated with liberal views. A lifelong teetotaler, he was surprised the first time I ordered a glass of wine when we were out to dinner. My move to the left paralleled his move to the right, so we were drawing farther apart. Generally, we avoided some topics of discussion.

That day on the couch, I used Sue's attempts at conversation to avoid going any further with Pappoo. I didn't want a theological disagreement to spoil our time together.

Soon the interview with Dr. Forbes ended, and Pappoo changed the channel.

Later that day, I went to hang out with some of my dearest friends from high school. Amie and I had met in fourth grade and had known each other all through our childhood and adolescence. Jason I met in seventh grade. In high school we hung out every day, sat at the same table at lunch, participated in group projects together for various classes, and spent many evenings playing ping pong and pool at my house. A mutual love of *Star Trek* bonded Jason and me.

We were close, but I wasn't quite ready to tell them about John or what I had decided about my sexuality. I wanted to explore all that on my own first before I began letting close friends know. So as we hung out that day, catching up, they primarily wanted to know about the girlfriend I had dated earlier in the year, who they hadn't had a chance to meet, and how that relationship had ended. I remember thinking, *This isn't even close to the most interesting thing going on in my life right now.*

Jason then started talking about my miserable record with women before turning to me and asking, "Have you tried being gay?"

I just smiled, and everyone else laughed.

Part of me wanted to scream out, "I will tomorrow!"

4

The Struggle Is Real

Lying prostrate on the floor, I prayed for direction. The hard wood pressed against my face and chest. My palms were sweaty from the exertion. This was the traditional position for contrition, and I wondered if it was sin that I was confessing. The discomfort seemed to focus my mind.

Between seeing John again in October and that Christmas with my family, I had struggled to understand my sexuality and whether I had the courage to take the risk necessary to live authentically. Unable to get John out of my mind, I took a day off from church for a private retreat. For hours I prayed, meditated, and reflected on the major decision confronting me.

Pondering the question of who I was, I ached with the desire to be held in the arms of a lover. I'd always assumed that would be a woman. Yet as long as I could remember, even back to childhood, my fantasies had been dominated by men. I had developed a strategy of avoidance. I acknowledged my same-sex desires to myself but chose not to act on them.

My ministry was thriving and my career prospects looked excellent. Friends and mentors were imagining a great future for me. *Why would I want to rock this boat?* I asked myself. My pastor's wife even told me she thought I was very talented, but she worried that something was going to happen to deny me the career I should have. I wonder if she anticipated what that would be.

Part of me wanted to settle the question of my attraction to men, for I had never seriously explored it. If I did, maybe I would learn whether being gay was my true self. My hangup was not the Bible or theology. My hangup that November day was my identity as a minister. Despite the fact that at the time I was working with somewhat more progressive religious people, I simply did not see how I could continue to be a minister as an openly gay man. And even if I could, the options seemed so limited. Was it worth forsaking a career I loved and was gifted at in order to pursue a sexual desire? Throwing the one away for the other seemed sinful to me, so I lay there prostrate on the floor, feeling like a character in a Sartre novel, trapped no matter what I chose.

I preached my first sermon on August 21, 1988 at the age of fourteen. While attending church camp that June, my youth minister asked me if I would preach for the upcoming "Youth Sunday." Of course I said yes, excited by this opportunity to fulfill the call I had experienced from the age of five.

The title of the sermon was "A Christian's Heritage as a Servant of the Lord." It was based on a passage from Isaiah 54, which includes lines like "O thou afflicted, tossed with tempest, and not comforted, behold, I will lay thy stones with fair colours, and lay thy foundations with sapphires." And "No weapon that is formed against thee shall prosper; and every tongue that shall rise against thee in judgment thou shalt condemn." The basic point of my sermon was that we suffer trials and temptations because of our difference, but if we are established in righteousness and obey God, then God will protect us.

Of course I look at it now and realize that this fits perfectly with a teenager who feels like an outsider. At the time I thought my difference was explained by my Christian piety and my call to ministry, so of course I would preach a sermon about Christians being different from the rest of the world.

I wrote the sermon pretty quickly after being asked that June, and then I rehearsed constantly. I erected a little stand in the living room, treating it as my pulpit. Every couple of days I'd stand there proclaiming at full voice, practicing gestures. *When should I move to the right? When do I need to look back at my notes? When should I lower my voice?*

After a few weeks of this, Mom asked the secretaries in the church office if she could bring me up to the church to rehearse, which they said I could do. When no one else was around, we'd walk into the darkened sanctuary that felt cavernous when empty. We'd turn on a few lights and then I'd stand behind the pulpit and practice. Much like in the picture I drew at five, there was Mom, sitting, watching, and giving me feedback.

If you were to ask Mom, she'd actually say she knew my destiny before I was born, though she didn't tell me until I was ordained at twenty-three.

When we returned home from the ordination service, filled with the honor and pride that such a special, sacred ceremony conveys, Mom sat me down in our living room and picked up her old Bible. The binding was broken from overuse and being stuffed with funeral programs, worship bulletins, and clippings from devotionals. She pulled out an envelope, slightly yellowed, and handed it to me. "I've been waiting for the right moment to give this to you, and I believe today is the day."

I was intrigued. Inside was a letter written by Mom to me back in 1981.

I was told by God that I was having a special child. I was carrying you at the time. I didn't know if the baby was going to be a boy or a girl, but it would be a special child. When I told my parents, they laughed at me and said all parents think that. I told them to just wait and see.

When you were five, you said God had called you to preach. You gave me the picture you had drawn at school of you preaching. It was then I prayed and asked God to tell me what he had in store for you. It was then he gave me the scriptures.

The letter included some scripture references, including one from the book of the prophet Jeremiah. God tells a young Jeremiah that God knew him in the womb and even there began to form him for his call to be a prophet to the nations.

As I finished reading the letter, sitting on our couch with the pastel floral pattern, I looked up to find Mom sitting patiently with a calm smile upon her face. I wasn't sure what to make of all this. It seemed overwhelming.

"I didn't tell you until today because I wanted your decision to be your own, not something you thought you had to do," she said softly. "It was obvious to me all of your life that God had his hand on you. Your childhood pastor noticed that you were different when you were five." There was conviction in her voice.

She told me that Ruth Robinson, my Sunday school teacher when I was four, came to visit her and said, "Who is this child? There's something special about him."

Mom smiled and nodded at the memory. "From then on I judged other people's faith based on if they saw it also."

I listened quietly as she shared my destiny. *Should I find this inspiring?* I wondered. *Or is it a set of expectations I might never fulfill?*

I hugged her, thanked her, and said, "I hope I can live up to all of this and make you proud."

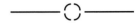

My mother was born in 1948, also in Miami, Oklahoma. She was the oldest of four children. Her Baby Boomer upbringing was recorded in old family films we watched on special occasions.

As a young woman she was petite, with curly blonde hair and blue eyes. She was actively courted by a handful of young men, my father among them. Dad's cousin introduced them to each other when they were eleven years old.

Mom was also very smart, something of a shining star in our hometown. She was a leader in school, church, and community organizations. As an adolescent, she worked for our local radio station. I heard often from older adults that my mother was well respected and admired.

As a smart, determined adolescent in the 1960s, she had felt called to the ministry herself. But the leaders at church explained to her that women could not be preachers. Because she was a champion in high school debate, she then considered the law, but was dissuaded from that as well because of her gender.

Like generations of smart women, she ended up becoming a schoolteacher. She was an excellent teacher, earning recognition even in her earliest years for incorporating new technologies and breaking new ground. In her late forties she completed her educational goals, receiving her doctorate from Oklahoma State University.

Turned away from full-time, professional ministry as an adolescent, Mom became a dedicated lay person. Early in their marriage, Mom and Dad served jointly as youth ministers, and throughout my childhood they either taught the youth group or the young adult class. We were at church almost every time the doors were opened.

I had many great experiences growing up in the church. The fun of summer camp on Grand Lake. The Sunday school teachers who loved me and taught me the skills they thought necessary for the good life. The moments during worship when I felt part of something large and meaningful.

But now I look back at those years with regret. I was endeavoring so hard to be the good kid, the person my church and the adults around me wanted me to be, that in the process, I didn't fully live.

Many people in that world are paranoid, afraid of those who are different. They are afraid of sex and body issues. They are so afraid of what their kids are going to do that the messages you hear as an adolescent are constantly negative: *Don't listen to this music, don't think those thoughts, don't associate with those kids.* We were taught the evils of rock music, how the Beatles had tried to lead children into disobedience and rebellion. Of course, we didn't listen to the Beatles; it was the 1980s.

Our generation did, however, listen to Madonna. And no one seemed to anger the religious sensibilities of the adults in my world more than Madonna and her intentional mocking of religious imagery. We had been warned about how dangerous her song "Like a Prayer" was, filled with sexual imagery and burning crosses. But I really liked that song; I knew all the words. When it played on the radio, I was tempted to sing along out loud, but I didn't. I was too afraid to be a sinner. But I'd sing along silently, wondering if I was courting damnation.

I try to give a charitable read to the ministers and church folk who taught me. They were well intentioned, kindhearted people who probably knew that most kids would only listen to them a little and then go ahead and do whatever they were going to do anyway.

What these teachers and leaders didn't realize, I don't think, is that for a kid trying as hard as he could to live up to everyone's expectations, a kid who really took this religion stuff seriously, those messages were suffocating. I took them to heart and constantly felt I wasn't good enough. I felt that there was something wrong with me.

Whenever I was asked to tell the story of my first kiss, I would tell about that time in kindergarten when Mrs. Hampton left the room momentarily and without warning, Kristie Holstein jumped up from her desk, rushed across the room, grabbed me, and planted a sloppy kiss on my lips. We ended up being boyfriend and girlfriend off and on through third grade.

But that sweet, innocent story isn't the truth. My first kiss was in Florence Rousseau's preschool Sunday school class at the First Baptist Church, when I kissed a boy.

He had sandy blonde hair and a pale complexion and for some reason in that moment, when we were playing with blocks, I felt overcome with affection for him and just like we did in our family, I demonstrated that feeling by playfully kissing him. Then some Sunday school teacher whose name I don't remember—despite the lasting influence she had on my development—said, "Bad men do that. Don't ever do it again."

It was a long, long time before I did. And I don't remember ever seeing that boy again.

I grew up with no resources to deal with my sexuality. Not just for dealing with being gay; even if I had been straight, my world had provided no messages other than the negative ones. If I got aroused, I felt guilty. I was a sinner. Then add to that the further confusion that my sexual fantasies were about guys.

One day when I was in the bathroom preparing to take a shower, I had an erection. Morning wood. Erections happened most mornings, and I had never thought anything of it. I just assumed it was a natural thing.

My dad came into the bathroom to get ready for work just as I was about to step into the shower. He saw my erection and asked me, "What's that?"

The way he asked the question, his stern tone of voice, conveyed that the erection was something bad. I was overcome with guilt and shame I hadn't had before.

"I don't know," I said. "Sometimes it's like that in the morning. I usually have to pee in the morning, too. Maybe that's why it's hard?"

Dad gave me a lecture about not masturbating. As a result, I never did. Oh, I played with myself in bed at night, but I never actually jacked off. I was cutting a fine line, but in the conflict between the fate of my eternal soul and my bodily pleasure, a fine line was what I had to walk.

One day in eighth grade I did something stupid. When we were home alone, I mentioned my struggles to my younger sister. I think I just needed to express them to someone, and I probably purposely picked someone who wouldn't understand what I was talking about. What an idiot I was! Erin only understood that I was talking about "naughty stuff," so she told Mom when she got home.

Mom found me in the family room watching TV and told me to come with her to her bedroom. She needed to talk to me. As we walked the hallway I noticed her slumped shoulders and the corners of her mouth turned down. After she closed the door she told me what Erin had told her.

"Have you talked to your father about this?" she asked.

"No, I can't. I'm too embarrassed," I answered.

Then, I spilled my guts to my mother—how my lusts were constant, how I played with myself in secret at night, how I found myself fantasizing about men. I asked her if these things were normal or if I was a sinner. I was hoping for some help, but there was no sympathy on her face.

"Are you gay?" she asked.

I didn't know how to answer that question. I'm not even sure that I understood exactly what the word meant. From what little I had learned on the subject, I knew it was a bad thing. I guess I answered in the negative, but I really don't remember what I said.

Mom said, "I can't handle you being gay. If you are gay, I will kill myself."

Once in graduate school, a friend asked me if I was gay. I answered, "I'm not. If I was gay, my mother would kill herself."

5

The Great Work Begins

"The administration knows that Sean is gay, and they are threatening to kick him out of school," Matt said as he entered our dorm room one afternoon in the autumn of 1993.

We were sophomores in ministry at Oklahoma Baptist University, a liberal arts college run by the Oklahoma branch of the Southern Baptist Convention. Homosexual activities were expressly forbidden in the code of conduct contained in the university handbook. I don't remember the exact wording of the policy, but I do remember that it came with a parenthesis filled with a long list of scriptural references.

Sean was a musician, a skilled trumpeter. He was not one of my close friends at college, but I knew him and had enjoyed his performances, and we had hung out on occasion. He and my roommate Matt were friends.

Sean was not out by any means. Few young people were in 1993, especially not in Oklahoma. That said, probably most people who knew Sean assumed or expected that he was gay. But as long as Sean never publicly acknowledged his orientation nor gave direct evidence of it, then he would be left alone by other students and by the university.

So how had the school learned he was gay? According to
the story that we pieced together in the ensuing days and
weeks, he had been turned in by the parents of one of our other
roommates. That roommate had grown up knowing Sean, and
their parents were friends. I've never known for certain if this
is precisely what happened, but that story shaped our lives. The
other roommate moved out of our suite that very week with no
explanation, rupturing what had been a tight group of friends.

Matt Cox and I had been matched as roommates our freshman year because of our similarities. He grew up in Tulsa and
had been a student leader in high school. His dad died at twenty-nine of colon cancer, and his mother had remarried when
Matt was young. His grandfather was a minister, and Matt
was following in his path. Like me, he was also a conservative
Republican. When Bill Clinton was proclaimed the victor of
the presidential election in November of our freshman year,
we immediately jumped up from our bunk beds where we had
been watching TV, took down the large American flag hanging
in our dorm room window and hung it upside down in the traditional symbol of the nation in distress. Later that week, the
university's president sent the head of the College Republicans
to ask us to turn the flag right side up.

That afternoon in our sophomore year when Matt first
shared the news about Sean, his face was flushed and his fists
were clenched. He was almost yelling.

"This is unacceptable," he said. "We can't let this happen. We
have to do something about it. We have to show some support
for Sean, challenge the administration in some way. What
should we do?"

I wasn't sure what to do, for this was one of the first times that my values were in conflict. I was a good kid who strove to live up to and exceed the expectations of the adults in my world, valuing their praise. I was generally someone who cooperated with authority and rarely got into trouble at school or at home.

Yet I also had a strong sense of right and wrong. No opportunity had yet appeared in my life to seriously challenge an injustice. Sure, in fourth grade I hung up some homemade posters on the school door expressing my anger that they were making us to go school on Memorial Day in order to make up for a lot of snow days that winter. The signs said, "Respect the Dead. No School on Memorial Day." I also created a handwritten petition on some notebook paper for other kids to sign. My mother, who taught in the school, saw what I was doing. She ripped the sign off the door, tore up the petition, and gave me a pretty good spanking.

So aside from my failed childhood effort at radicalism, if I chose to challenge the university, this would be new ground for me.

When I arrived at Oklahoma Baptist University in August of 1992 as an eighteen-year-old conservative, Southern Baptist preacher boy, I thought I knew quite a bit. I had been a straight-A student in high school, and I'd spent my entire childhood and adolescence raised in church. I was excited to learn, but was confident that I had the basics covered, especially about the Bible.

My first class was Introduction to the Old Testament with Dr. Rick Byargeon. Dr. Byargeon always wore tailored suits, except on test days when he would appear in jeans and an OBU sweatshirt. Though he was a tough teacher, he was the best lecturer I've ever had. His sections always closed first during enrollment.

Dr. Byargeon's tests were notorious for being incredibly difficult. One day some student in our class asked, "How do we prepare for the test?"

Dr. Byargeon answered, "Memorize the lecture outlines."

We all thought that was a rather annoying response until we saw the first test. One of the questions was something like, "Reproduce the outline for the lecture entitled 'Covenant in the Book of Exodus.'"

His final exam was comprehensive and could, therefore, ask anything about the entire Old Testament. One question I remember distinctly, because I had no clue to the answer, was "Name the sons of Eli." Now after years of ordained ministry, I still couldn't name the sons of Eli, nor can I imagine why anyone would care.

Those tough tests were still unknown to me that first week of university, as I gathered with the other freshmen students for the eight a.m. class. I took a spot near the back of the room so that I could observe the entire class during discussions, something that became a habit for me. I was eager for my college education to begin, and more importantly, for my formal education in religion to commence. I was embarking upon the next phase in my call to Christian ministry.

As he began to lecture that day and throughout the semester, Dr. Byargeon opened a wider world for me. I was to learn that

I knew far less than I had thought. My Sunday school education in the Bible, no matter how good it was, just didn't prepare me for everything I was going to learn about critical, scholarly methods of interpreting scripture.

I have described my freshman year this way: I entered with my worldview built upon a solid foundation nurtured by my family and childhood faith, and my professors took sledgehammers to that foundation and destroyed it. I then spent a couple of years trying to piece something back together, until I finally realized that I could only build a raft to keep myself afloat, and that the pieces of that raft would be constantly changing.

For instance, there was the day later in the year when I was driving back to my childhood home three hours away after a particularly challenging philosophy class. As I drove along the interstate through the central hills and woods of Oklahoma, I was processing all I was learning in that class and others. As I reasoned, I argued myself out of belief in a literal Adam and Eve. And I was frightened. For I realized that this belief was only one piece crumbling from a foundation that probably wouldn't hold together.

Now I laugh at how ignorant and provincial I was. In the years to come I would encounter a Christian tradition that was both broader and deeper than I had ever imagined, discovering that it had room for all my doubts and my questions and that what was awaiting me was a more vibrant, open, and adventurous spirituality. Looking back now on the intellectual explorations of those collegiate years, I remember the time as joyful and exciting because I was constantly learning and remaking myself. Even if it didn't always feel that way in the moment.

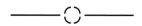

The afternoon Matt had sprung the news about Sean, I paced my dorm room, mulling over what I would do, if anything. Since the room wasn't that wide or long, the pacing was pretty intense. As my values and personality traits clashed, I carried on quite an internal dialogue.

Should I help defend Sean and stand up against what my gut tells me are 'un-Christian' actions of the administration? I wondered. I knew that doing so might threaten my reputation or even my position in the university. If I spoke out, my plans to be a minister could be damaged. *And would people think that I'm gay?* If they did, I knew the school might kick me out, too.

Even as I paced frantically, this felt like a defining moment. I was now an adult, responsible for shaping my own character. I had to decide what sort of person I wanted to be. Once I phrased the question that way, the answer came quickly. I could not live with myself if I backed down from defending what I knew to be right.

Though at nineteen I still held very conservative views of homosexuality, believing that it was a sin, I knew that what the school was doing to Sean was not fair and was definitely not the loving grace of Jesus Christ. So I took the chance and decided to support him.

That evening, three of us met with the Dean of Students to express our dismay. The Dean's office was on the second floor of the Student Union. We walked there anxiously, unsure of what would happen.

On the dark, wood-paneled walls of his office, the Dean's

diplomas hung among framed photos of the school. He politely welcomed us in and placed an extra chair beside his desk. He sat down and leaned forward, crossing his arms on the desktop, and asked us why we were there.

Matt led the conversation. "We are friends with Sean Baugh," he began. "We understand that the university is threatening to kick him out of school because of a rumor that he is gay."

I don't think the Dean was expecting that news. He sat back, clearly mulling over how to proceed.

"You understand that I cannot discuss confidential issues of other students, right?" he said. His voice, as always, was measured and calm.

"Yes, we are aware of that," Matt said. "But Sean himself has told us. We are here to state our support for Sean and our disagreement with the school's actions towards him."

The Dean breathed deeply and moved a pen on his desk. "Let me say first that at this time no action has been taken against Sean," he said, "so there is nothing for you to register a complaint about. Second, the policy of this university on the issue of homosexuality is very clear. It is not an accepted lifestyle choice, and homosexual activities are banned by the student code of conduct, which all students agree to upon enrolling in the university."

He paused to let this information sink in before continuing, "If we were to find that a student was engaging in homosexual activities, then it is our duty to deal with that situation the same as if we caught a young man and a young woman having sex, or if a student was drunk."

"But Sean wasn't caught doing anything on campus," Matt said fervently. He was expressing a concern we had discussed before the meeting. "So I am confused how the policy operates in this situation."

I was eager for the Dean's response. He looked at each of us in turn before he responded.

"The student code of conduct is not simply how we expect students to behave while on campus. It is binding on students in the university even if they are not on campus."

I found this confusing. I could tell Matt did, too. He raised his eyebrows spoke a little louder, leaning forward in his chair. "So you mean that if a student is drinking while home on summer vacation, say, or a boyfriend and girlfriend are having sex at an apartment away from the school, that is a violation of the university's policy and that in those situations you bring disciplinary action?"

The Dean shifted in his chair. "We would deal compassionately and fairly, but we must also uphold the university's rules and the teachings of God. Correct?"

It didn't take a lot of smarts to realize that even if this was the school's policy, the administration clearly wasn't enforcing the policy this way. If they did, there would be no end to the disciplinary actions taken against students. We weren't Bob Jones University, after all, but a liberal arts school that valued (and trumpeted) its high annual rankings on the *U. S. News & World Report* list of colleges and universities.

I finally spoke up. "While we can agree that homosexuality is a sin, clearly threatening to expel a student is not the loving and gracious approach that we, as Christians, should take."

The Dean smiled. "This is a difficult situation. What is the loving response? Is the loving response to allow someone to continue in sinful behavior or to challenge that sin, hopefully leading to repentance?"

There was silence in the room. He continued.

"My advice to you as friends of Sean's would be to pray for him and help him. Now I really must get home to my wife and children."

As we departed, he politely thanked us for coming in, and closed the door behind us. We were in a somber mood as we slowly walked back across the campus to our dorm.

No threat to the three of us transpired, but the school informed Sean that for him to remain enrolled in the university, he would have to cease homosexual activities and go to a counselor to help him overcome these tendencies. The counseling was a form of reparative therapy that evangelicals at the time hoped would alter people's sexual orientation.

I was still years away from dealing openly with my own sexuality. It was like a phantom lingering around the edges of my life, and now I felt the need to be even more cautious. Further, I was sad that my decision to speak up, which took such conscious effort, didn't appear to result in any change in the university.

A year later, Sean was the victim of a hate crime, beaten up while in Oklahoma City's gay neighborhood one night. As he lay in his hospital bed recovering from this gay bashing, he received word from the university that he was being kicked out of school with only a semester to go before graduation. This crime and its location where the evidence that he was unrepentant.

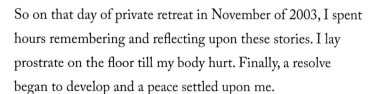

So on that day of private retreat in November of 2003, I spent hours remembering and reflecting upon these stories. I lay prostrate on the floor till my body hurt. Finally, a resolve began to develop and a peace settled upon me.

That afternoon, I wrote in my journal:

Is this my "dark night of the soul"? Am I being called to a difficult experience or task? Could this, in itself, be transforming for me and others?

The idea of call itself, the thing that had always been the stumbling block, was now finally allowing me to seriously consider exploring my sexual attraction for John. Was it possible that my sexual identity was connected to the work that God was calling me to? That question was radically new for me and was a promising question to consider.

I left that day of private retreat feeling renewed and joyful. If I hadn't had plans that night, I probably would have called John and told him everything. Instead, I went to see two of the teenagers from church play football. All through the game I was bursting with excitement.

But that night I awoke frightened. *I can't do this,* I told myself. *What was I thinking?* I was relieved that I hadn't yet done anything stupid.

The fear and anxiety persisted for a few more conflicted weeks until HBO aired the film version of Tony Kushner's *Angels in America*—the story of a group of people living in New York in the 1980s in the midst of the AIDS crisis. One of them, Joe, was a very good-looking young Mormon man who was wrestling with his attraction to men and what his sexual orientation might mean for his career in conservative politics, his marriage to his wife, his relationship to his mother, and his faith. Over the course of the two weeks that the six-part film aired, I found myself identifying with the character of Joe and being drawn into the rich themes of the story.

At the end of those two weeks, I was home alone watching the final episode, sitting on my couch. In the closing scene, some of the major characters meet at the Bethesda Fountain in Central Park. Joe is not there, having been unable to embrace his sexuality and hold the various pieces of his identity together. But his mother Hannah is, having made the journey herself to a new understanding. Then Prior Walter, who has AIDS and functions as the Prophet in the story, speaks directly into the camera, giving a benediction. He says that our time has come and that we are fabulous. He ends the benediction, "The Great Work begins."

He was speaking to me. I stood up from the couch and knew, finally, that I had the courage to do this.

6

Tums

So, fast forward to that evening after Christmas when John and I were sitting beside each other on my living room couch watching *The Lord of the Rings: The Two Towers*. About halfway through the film I paused the DVD, turned to him, and said, "I want to explore the possibility of a relationship with you."

Then, I gave a speech that lasted almost an hour. I explained my sexual history (isn't that a great way to start a relationship?), my confusion and excitement, my worries about the future (surely that inspires confidence in the object of one's affection), my desires and what had happened since I'd seen him last. I asked him if he wanted to take all that on, with all the risk. Because if so, I told him, I wanted us to explore that possibility together.

He sat there through it all, patiently, occasionally asking a question, laughing at something I'd said, or smiling gently. And, then, with it all laid out there and the step finally taken, I waited for his response.

"Yes," he said. "I do want to explore that possibility. But do you have any Tums?"

"What?"

"Do you have any Tums? I'm so nervous that I'm sick to my stomach. I need Tums." He looked nervous, but also happy.

"No, I don't have any Tums," I said, a little exasperated that this moment was turning absurd.

So we drove to CVS for some Tums. John drove. He was steering with his left hand, so I reached over and touched the back of his right hand. He turned it palm up, and we held hands. The intimate contact with his flesh felt so good and right; in that moment, so many anxieties melted away.

"I've had a crush on you, you know, for three years," John said, looking over at me as we were on our way back from the drugstore and after he'd taken the Tums. "Over the last couple of months I've suspected that something was going on with you. Once you asked me to stay this weekend, I was pretty sure what was going to happen. And you confirmed it tonight at dinner."

"At dinner?" I was intrigued. "What did I do at dinner?"

"I moved my leg over against yours so that our knees were touching, and you didn't move your leg. A guy not interested would have moved his leg."

"Oh, how funny," I laughed. "I hadn't even thought about it. I remember our legs touching. It's funny, I didn't decide in that moment not to move mine, I just didn't move it."

"Exactly." We smiled at each other.

As he turned onto my street, he sat up straighter and said, "One more thing. I've also got a surprise for you, something I think you'll like."

"Oh, what's that?" I asked.

"Two weeks ago I started quitting smoking," he said. "I know you don't smoke and probably didn't like that I smoked, so I decided that just in case this is where things were headed, I'd go ahead and quit."

I was pleasantly surprised. "Wow," I said. "So you really had figured out what was going on with me." John's announcement overwhelmed me. Despite the Tums emergency, this was going so well.

As he pulled into my driveway, he said, "But I really want a cigarette right now. I'm pretty nervous, so I'm going to smoke."

He pulled a pack of cigarettes out of his glove box and we stood in the driveway as he smoked. Suddenly he turned, bent over, and threw up beside the car.

"Oh, my," I said, in complete shock. "Are you okay? Let me go get you some water."

"Well, that's fucking embarrassing," John said, wiping his lips with the back of his hand.

"Maybe something you ate didn't sit right?" I offered.

He shook his head. "No, I think I'm just that nervous." He took another draw on the cigarette.

When he finished smoking, we went back inside. He brushed his teeth and then returned to the living room, where I walked up to him and kissed him. I had never kissed someone taller than me before. Kissing looking up was strangely and wonderfully different. And his whiskers—I'd never kissed anyone with whiskers before. He had a goatee, and the moustache tickled a little bit.

We cuddled on the couch. Eventually I said, "Take me to the bedroom."

7

Behind the Outlet Mall

After that weekend, I called Matt, my old college roommate.

"I'm dating someone," I announced.

"Okay," he answered, seeming somewhat confused as to why I had called for the first time in months and jumped immediately into this news.

"His name is John." I grinned as I said it.

Matt sighed. "I never thought you'd have the balls to do it."

Matt was gay. But he'd dealt with it years ago. A few months after he and I had fought the school over Sean's expulsion, he told me he'd been struggling with his own sexual orientation.

I'd had a complex emotional reaction to that news, a reaction I didn't fully understand in the moment. Part of me desired the opportunity to explore same-sex attraction and sexuality with him, while other parts of me recoiled in fear that the proximity of Matt's struggle would make my own that much more difficult. I was envious of him and also ashamed at my own lack of courage.

Over the next year and a half, Matt went in and out of the closet, trying to reconcile his faith and sexuality. Finally, on a college choir tour, he became involved with the man who became his husband. They had been together almost a decade when I made my call to tell Matt I finally had a boyfriend. We had walked the journey of his coming out together; now that I was finally coming out, I wanted him to be the first to know.

I came out to others slowly at first. The closet, as I later came to understand, can be a nurturing womb as you initially explore your identity and learn new things about yourself. But stay inside too long and it becomes a prison, blocking your access to light and life. Even within the first few weeks of the relationship with John, I began to feel both aspects.

The secret weighed more heavily on me at certain times, especially when I felt compelled to lie. For example, I spent New Year's Eve with young adult friends from church. I was the only single guy present, so they all started talking about fixing me up and wanted to know what I was attracted to in a woman. I felt guilty at not being forthright and honest.

Later in January, I came out to two other close friends. One was overcome with joy for me. The other was a ministry colleague who understood the complexities ahead. Both confessed that they had always wondered if I was gay and simply not in touch with my own identity.

These conversations were preparation for telling my sister, who I considered my best friend. She was coming to Dallas to hang out for a weekend at the end of the month, and I looked forward to telling her then.

Erin is three years younger than me, and I had doted on her from the moment she appeared in my life. Mom enjoys telling the story of how I would crawl into Erin's baby bed, having sneaked crackers she wasn't supposed to have any more of, and

Mom would find us curled up asleep together in the baby bed with crumbs all over the place.

Erin was probably always a bit more ambivalent about being a little sister. Mom liked to tell a story from when Erin was a toddler. I was lying on the living room floor napping, when she came riding by on her tricycle and chose to ride over my head instead of going around. Mom thought the story was revealing about Erin's attitude to her big brother.

Having spent all of her growing-up years being referred to by teachers and other adults as "Scotty's little sister," Erin surprised everyone when she chose to come to Oklahoma Baptist University as well, with her freshman year and my senior year overlapping. Since I continued to live in the same town for graduate school, I was there throughout her college years. During that time we developed a close bond and became friends, not simply siblings.

I was very happy when she married Adam. He was a gentle and caring guy, close to his family, with a professional career. He also enjoyed sports and having a good time. Adam and I enjoyed talking about football and golf.

I had no worries about coming out to Erin. She knew Matt and the various other gay friends I had acquired in college. Plus, she had been close friends with a gay guy in her class; they sometimes escorted each other to dances and parties.

We met up in Frisco, about fifteen miles north of where I lived in Dallas. She gave me a big hug and said she wanted to go shopping at the outlet mall in Allen, which was about fifteen minutes away.

I was eager to share my good news, so moments after we got

in the car I said with excitement, "I've got good news that I'm excited to share with you."

"Oh, what's that?" she asked, an inquisitive arch to her eyebrows.

"I'm dating someone." I was smiling as I looked over at her and she grinned back. "His name is John."

In that moment all the life and joy and sparkle drained from her eyes. Her face turned white. She grabbed the door handle and began heaving. "Pull over. I'm going to be sick."

We were on a highway, but fortunately the road had wide shoulders. As I rolled to a stop, she threw open the door and rushed from the car into the grass beside the road and doubled over quaking.

I knew enough to stay in the car.

After a few minutes, during which she never got sick, she returned to the car. And then she turned on me.

"But you always denied it whenever anyone asked you if you were," she almost yelled at me. "And all these years whenever anyone asked me if you were, I always defended you and said that you weren't. You've made a liar out of me. How could you do that?"

I felt like I had driven headlong into a wall. "But Erin, I was struggling with it for all these years and never could face the truth about myself. Either that or I lacked the courage, especially being a minister."

She was silent, so I started driving again. "I'm sorry," I said. "I didn't think you'd react this way. I would have found another way to tell you. I just assumed it wouldn't be a big deal for you. That you'd be happy for me. That you'd want to hear all about it." I was imploring her to let this be true.

"Why would you ever think that?" she almost spat the words at me.

"Why? Because you're my sister." I couldn't believe the nightmare the conversation had turned into.

"I'm so disgusted with you right now. Just leave me alone," she said. And so we drove in silence, with her staring out the window, away from me.

Not knowing what else to do, I went ahead and stopped at the outlet mall. As we parked, she said, still not looking at me, "I need some space. Leave me alone." Then she got out of the car and walked away.

I couldn't even cry. I was so shocked and confused. Eventually I got out of the car and went to the bathroom and washed my face.

When I came out of the men's room, Erin was exiting the women's. "I have something to tell you," she said.

"Okay," I indicated an exit that led to the backside of the outlet mall. "Let's go out here."

She followed me outside the door to the back area of the mall, where discarded cigarettes littered the ground and the air conditioners roared

She didn't look at me as she began to speak. "I can't handle any of this. I'm so ashamed. I don't want to see you or talk to you. I called Adam, and he is on his way to get me. We are going back home. Don't call me. And when I have children, I don't want you near them." With that, she walked through the door and back inside, not giving me any chance to respond.

And in that moment, standing behind an outlet mall, I felt

cast in my own Nineties independent dramedy, like something directed by Richard Linklater. But it was me instead of Ethan Hawke or John Cusack, and my sister instead of Christina Ricci or Winona Ryder. It was absurd, how I was feeling. I wanted to move on to the next scene.

8

"I don't know what they could handle."

I began writing my sister letters. In the first one, I said that the problem was clear to me—we did not know each other. All these years we'd thought we did. But if she wasn't prepared for my news, and I wasn't prepared for how she would take it, clearly we had just assumed we knew one another. So I wrote her letters telling her all about myself. One letter I entitled "The Mythos of a Gen-X Male."

In the late Seventies and early Eighties, there was a series of films that defined my childhood and thus my life. They gave us, especially guys my age, a feeling for adventure and a sense that life did and could contain something greater. What I'm saying is that these formed the mythos of my life and my group of guy friends.

The pantheon of these films is represented by my three all-time favorites:

1 The Empire Strikes Back

2 E.T.

3 Indiana Jones & the Raiders of the Lost Ark

But there has been a problem with these being our myths. Our

*lives didn't end up being full of adventure. There is a sense that
Lucas & Spielberg lied to us.*

After the first letter, she e-mailed and told me not to send
her any more. I ignored her and kept on writing.

I didn't come out to anyone else for a while after that.
Instead, I focused my energies on my relationship with John.
I was falling in love.

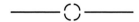

John and I talked on the phone every evening at 9 p.m. We
discussed *American Idol* (this was the Fantasia and Jennifer
Hudson season), David Sedaris, and *Sex in the City*. Sharing
stories, we soon realized we had probably encountered one
another when we were adolescents. John had grown up a
Southern Baptist preacher's kid, living in various small towns
in Oklahoma. During the summers his family worked at our
state church camp, Falls Creek.

Falls Creek is quite the institution in Oklahoma. The campground is situated in the Arbuckle Mountains in the south central region of the state—yes, there are mountains in Oklahoma.
The road we took to get there was narrow and curvy, with views
down the side of the mountain. Getting to camp in big buses
and touring coaches, I was always afraid we were going to top-
ple off the side of the road. And there were cacti. They always
seemed so alien to me, because we did not have any in northeastern Oklahoma. I always imagined that if the bus toppled off
the road, I'd land in a huge pile of thorny cacti.

Six thousand kids attended camp each week. Almost every
teenager growing up in Oklahoma, even if they weren't a

Baptist, at least had a chance to attend camp at Falls Creek. Rumor abounded that Falls Creek was one of the reasons Oklahoma's teen pregnancy rate was so high. Which was paradoxical, because the camp had a strict dress code. You couldn't wear shorts unless they went below your knees (which is why Oklahoma Southern Baptists were really into the Jams craze in the late Eighties). Guys had to wear slacks to worship, and girls had to wear dresses or skirts. And the tabernacle, where those thousands of people worshiped every evening, fully clothed, was open and not air conditioned.

John's family worked the concession stand. Pretty much every day of camp, you'd walk down to the concession stand in your khakis and buy something cold to fight the oppressive heat. John might have sold me a snow cone or an ice cream sandwich.

The other time we might have met was when John was in high school and was part of the state Baptist youth choir the same year my sister was. That year they toured in Texas, and I just happened to catch the concert at the Riverwalk in San Antonio. I was in San Antonio with my girlfriend for a visit with her grandparents.

John and I would laugh over these stories—our *Mad About You* moments, referencing the television show whose romantic leads had a series of childhood encounters recalled at times during the series.

I liked running my hands through the hair on the back of his head. And showering together. No one had ever told me how much fun that would be.

When he came to visit over Valentine's Day weekend, I had prepared a romantic evening. He arrived to find all the lights off and votive candles leading the way to the bedroom, where I had rose petals spread all over. On the nightstand was a bottle of champagne, cheese, chocolates, and fruit.

"I thought we could eat dinner in bed," I said.

During his Dallas visits that spring, we'd go to the movies and Half Price Books. We didn't hang out with any of my local friends, for none of them yet knew about my being gay.

I was surprised when he first told me he had never come out to his parents, though he knew that everyone in the family knew he was gay. He decided it was finally time to have an open conversation with them about it. His mom cried, mainly because she was relieved that he finally shared it. They were happy that he was dating me, having met me when I performed Sarah's wedding, and were excited to welcome me into their home and family. When I told Sarah how my sister had reacted, she said, "If your family abandons you, ours will be there for you."

So I visited him in Edmond and stayed at his parents' home. During one of those visits in early March, we were sitting in John's car outside his parents' house. We had just kissed and I had leaned back in my seat, content.

"Now I know what everyone else has been talking about all these years," I said. John looked at me as I stroked his hand and continued. "This is so much more powerful than anything I've ever experienced. I thought I'd experienced passion before, but I hadn't. I thought I'd experienced love before, but I hadn't. I don't even recognize myself with you."

Royal Lane Baptist Church sits grandly at the intersection of Hillcrest Avenue and Royal Lane in a North Dallas neighborhood of sprawling ranch-style homes with broad lawns and large picture windows. The architecture is Colonial—red brick, white columns, tall steeple, and clear glass windows through which one could sit on a Sunday morning and meditate on the patterns created by the branches of the oaks spreading outside.

I moved to Dallas in 2003 to start my new job as Associate Pastor for Youth and Education. I had been serving as a youth minister at a church in Fayetteville, Arkansas, and I hadn't been looking for a job. I knew Ray Vickery and Harry Wooten, the pastor and music minister at Royal Lane, from our years of attending the same summer camp with our youth groups. They became convinced I was the person they wanted to be their next youth minister. They tried for months to persuade me to visit the church before I finally agreed. I always thought Dallas represented everything wrong with America—right-wing politics, congestion, suburban sprawl, and mass consumption. But once I visited the church, I fell in love with it. I even eventually came to love Dallas.

Ray Vickery had been the pastor of Royal Lane for more than twenty years. He had just turned seventy. He had been a champion runner in college and retained the trimness and vigor of a much younger man. His bearing was both authoritative and charming; he smiled broadly. He was over six feet tall with bright white hair that was always perfectly combed. Distinguished is an overused word, but the word fit Ray.

Ray was a respected Baptist statesman. He had endured the Eighties-era fights in the Southern Baptist Convention and was a leader in the moderate and progressive camp. Other ministers treated him with deference and sometimes awe.

Harry was in his late forties; he was tall, with curly brown hair and an Arkansas Delta accent. He was a gifted music director, skilled at planning worship and leading a choir. Working with Harry was like taking graduate-level seminars in hymnody and worship design.

Ray, Harry, and I were a dream team. We worked very well together and rarely had disagreements. We spent many hours each week in collaboration. Not only did we have weekly staff meetings and worship planning meetings, one or two days a week we would go out for lunch or happy hour together. Our favorite place was the Bavarian Grill, a great German beer hall surprisingly located in a Plano strip mall. When we were doing it up right, we'd arrive after the lunch rush for our own late lunch of trout, red cabbage, spinach, and pretzel rolls washed down by Warsteiner Dunkel, all served by Greta in her Bavarian attire. After lunch we'd smoke a cigar and then eventually order Black Forest cake and coffee for dessert. We'd usually leave about the time the dinner crowd was beginning to arrive. Sometimes we'd actually plan an entire season of worship during one of these outings. Other times it was just fellowship.

Though I was a member of the Cooperative Baptist Fellowship, the moderate group of Baptists who had broken away from the Southern Baptist Convention, the Fellowship was divided between the progressive folks and the more traditional moderates. At its annual meeting in 2001, the General Assembly had voted on a resolution that was our first look at how the denomination felt on gay issues. The national governing council enacted a policy that barred hiring LGBT persons at the national office.

The vote had been close, and controversy ensued. Many in the Fellowship felt the decision was eerily similar to the discriminatory policies of the Southern Baptist Convention we had all so recently abandoned. An effort arose to overturn the discriminatory policy at the annual General Assembly, when representatives of the entire Fellowship could vote. After much debate, the effort to overturn the anti-gay policy received forty percent of the vote. Though many of the most liberal members of the Fellowship were disheartened—some of those left the fledgling group at that time—others, like me, felt that a forty percent pro-gay vote on our first effort was pretty good and that it was therefore worth staying and trying to effect change.

There were some signs that made me feel hopeful that I could come out and remain at Royal Lane. Ray had been one of the leaders in a movement attempting to open more dialogue on the topic of homosexuality. Also, Royal Lane had prominent gay and lesbian members serving in leadership roles. When I arrived at Royal Lane in the winter of 2003 and met these individuals, I finally discovered people like me—educated professionals who were active churchgoers and in long-term relationships. Their example empowered me, for I saw that I might have the same life.

But I also knew that Ray was cautious. He didn't like grand gestures and moved very slowly on controversial issues. He also came from an older school of ministry which said that ministers should not try to be friends with their congregants and should not open up about their own issues.

Ray had already cautioned me in the past about being too open regarding things far less sensitive than my sexuality.

That spring, I decided to test the waters and come out to Harry. We had grown personally close in the year I had served at Royal Lane. His family had pretty much adopted me as another member. They even gave me a Wooten name. Since all the children's names began with B, I became "Beaux Wooten" after I told them that one name my dad had considered for me was Bo Deacon Jones. The Wootens chose the more sophisticated spelling.

Harry and I were driving back from a meeting in Fort Worth late one night when I opened up with him.

"Harry, I'm dating someone." I spoke with more calm restraint than I had used months before when I came out to people, having now learned the risks involved. "His name is John."

"Oh?" he said, turning slightly toward me with what appeared to be a controlled grin. "When did this happen?"

"We began dating just after Christmas. You've met him. He visited church that weekend."

Harry seemed to think for a moment before commenting. "Ah. I do remember the guy you are talking about. He's cute."

"Thanks." I appreciated the note of solidarity in the midst of his very measured response.

"So, how did this come about?"

As we drove through the nighttime traffic, I shared the story of seeing John back in October and what had transpired since, as I struggled to come to terms with my sexuality. He listened attentively, interrupting now and then with a question or an encouraging word.

"Scott, I am so happy for you," he said, beaming at me.

"Thank you, Harry. I knew you would be." I was glad my intuition had been correct this time.

After a few minutes' silence, he said, without turning, "Have you thought about church and your career?"

"Yes, of course. Quite a bit." I had also expected this turn of the conversation, for Harry was cautious about anything that might cause conflict.

"You don't want to take anything too quickly. You need to spend time thinking about it before you make any moves."

"Yes, I know." And I knew his caution was a kindness.

"For instance, it is probably best to keep things pretty quiet for right now."

"I agree. I'm still exploring things myself." I told him about coming out to my sister and how her reaction had warned me off moving more quickly.

"Good," he said. "Have you told anyone from the church?" The way he spoke, I knew he had been working toward this question.

"No, I haven't."

"Not even any of the other gay guys or the young adults you are friends with?" he probed further.

"Not yet, no," I answered. He nodded and seemed assured.

Then I added, "It's been difficult, actually, keeping it from them. I'm ashamed of not being forthright and honest."

"I understand, but that's best for now." Again, I knew his caution was a kindness; this situation could complicate things for all of us.

Harry continued. "Enjoy your relationship and explore your

identity. But don't make any sudden public moves." I understood what he was saying, but I also needed to discuss the ethical quandary I was in.

So I persisted, "It's really difficult at times, being so guarded and secretive. It's not my normal way of doing ministry. I like to be open."

He grinned slightly, "And yet you've kept your struggle with your sexuality a secret all these years, so you do know how to do it."

What he said cut deeply at my sense of integrity, but he was right about my hypocrisy.

"I guess you're right," I responded. "But I'm not proud of that. I feel as if I lacked integrity."

"Scott," and now his tone was fatherly in nature, "standing up for your principles is good, but it can also be dangerous. You have to choose wisely. If you came out right now, your career would end. You need to think about that."

"I understand," I said. And I did. I knew I wasn't ready to expose myself to that risk.

Then I asked, "You don't think Royal Lane is ready? You don't think they could handle my coming out?"

"I don't know what they could handle," Harry sighed. "I've learned from many years of experience that churches rarely handle controversies well. Some people would be very supportive and others would be very upset. I do know a public fight wouldn't be good for the church or for you personally."

We drove along in silence for a while. I was pondering Harry's advice when he turned and said, "Please promise me one thing. Don't tell Ray anytime soon."

"Okay, I won't." That promise seemed easy.

"Good. And if at any point you plan to tell him, please let me know first."

"Of course. I will do that," I assured my friend.

The lights of the Dallas skyline loomed ahead.

9

When It Don't Come Easy

While on a church ski trip to Colorado over Spring Break, I wrote in my journal:

I need to figure out how to be less earnest in my relationships and not feel the need for "this" to be the relationship that works. That said, things with John are good. I just don't want to rush it or drive John away or add to his stress.

I was hoping John would surprise me and come to Dallas when I returned from the ski trip, but he didn't. He was too busy with work.

The next weekend, I drove to Oklahoma to visit him. We helped one of his co-workers move. John seemed distracted; he said he was stressed. I was glad when we finally had the chance to make out a bit in his parents' driveway, feeling like teenagers. He only had to touch me and my entire body tingled.

On April 4, he didn't answer when I called for our usual 9 p.m. phone call. I didn't think anything of it, as we didn't always connect every night.

Journal entry for April 7, 2004:

I've been growing increasingly concerned over the last month and especially the last week about the energy John is putting forth in the relationship. I think he is weighed down by work currently. But the lack of actually talking over the last three days deeply concerns me.

April 9:

John has not returned any of my calls. I feel the impending doom now. Even if it is possible that he has no problem with me or us, I do now. But I'm sure there is some problem—there has to be a motivation for this.

April 10:

Yesterday I got an email from John. He is needing time to figure out some things about himself and us. But he still loves me and still wants the relationship. But I don't know what the relationship is at this point. I don't think it can be worked through in a vacuum. I don't understand how he could need time or space. This is a long-distance relationship, and we didn't see each other for a month before last week. I will not be treated this way.

April 26:

Despite my best efforts not to think about it, I can't help it. It is destroying me slowly.

May 10:

Everything in the relationship came to a head last week. John got angry at a phone message I left. I got angry at his e-mail. He's supposed to call me on Wednesday to make arrangements for us meeting to talk all this out. I don't know what to do or what we should do. Are we right for each other at this point in our lives? There is this really powerful feeling of love for him. I just don't know what to do.

May 12:

He didn't call. That means it's over. The problem is, I still love him. And I still don't think that it had to happen this way.

In March I'd bought tickets for John and I to see The Indigo Girls. All the other young adult couples in the church were going. I knew that taking John along on this group date would make our relationship obvious to all of them. That also was part of the excitement. John was looking forward to going, as he had never seen The Indigo Girls live. Nor had I, even though they'd been a favorite band of mine since high school.

The concert was in late April. As the date approached, I didn't hear from John. He never actually backed out of going, but he never finalized plans to be in Dallas that weekend. At the last minute, I asked one of the single, straight guys from church if he wanted to use my extra ticket. At the concert, it seemed like everyone around me was with someone else. They were holding hands and kissing. And here I was, by myself, pushed up against the railing by a strange couple in front of me who kept insisting on getting more and more in my space and then glowering at me if I tried to get any room. What I had hoped to be a celebratory event—a romantic night with my boyfriend to see a favorite band—was miserable.

Months later, when I finally heard from him, John revealed that he had become anxious. The relationship was moving too fast, he said. I was too intense. He claimed that I was also sexually aggressive. That last one surprised me, for we had never had sexual intercourse, despite my desire for it.

I realize now that in many ways John served a function in my life, playing that key role of the person who facilitated my coming out. But once I started coming out, I wanted to live fully into my new identity. I didn't want to waste any more time. I just assumed, wrongly it turned out, that he would be open to that and would be able to provide the nurturing and guidance I needed at that point in my life.

Understanding all of that a decade later, I still think he could have ended things better. He never actually broke up with me. He simply quit calling. This person I had fallen for had suddenly abandoned me. I had risked everything for this relationship. I'd already lost my sister, the person who I had previously felt closest to in the entire world. Very few of my closest friends were aware of what was going on. Plus, I had been experiencing so much joy and delight in learning all sorts of new things about myself, exploring my identity as a gay man, and suddenly all of that ended. I was an emotional wreck.

To further complicate things, for the months that followed, I never quit loving John, no matter how angry and hurt I was. That summer, Harry's wife said to me, "You've simply got to quit caring for him. It's not healthy."

"I know, I know," I said. "But I just can't seem to quit."

I became a depressed person. I was irritable. Having trouble with the copy machine one day in the church office, I screamed and threw a bunch of papers all over the place, in front of one of the secretaries, and stomped out as she stared in shocked dismay.

Another day at the office, I found myself unable to function. So I emailed my secretary, who was sitting just outside my door, and told her I was not feeling well and was going home. I left by the side door, went home, and lay in bed all day listening to sad music and crying.

In May I discovered Patty Griffin's album *Impossible Dream* and kept listening to the song "When It Don't Come Easy" about how love goes through difficult moments.

Some of the more intuitive laypeople sensed that something was wrong. I learned later, for instance, that one congregant, upon running into the girlfriend who had broken up with me the autumn before, told her that she had really hurt me. Much later, I learned that she was a little angry when she learned the truth.

And as if I wasn't overwhelmed enough, my plumbing started leaking. First the trap on the master bathroom toilet. When I replaced that, I realized the in-flow mechanism was leaking. When I fixed that, the hose connecting the toilet to the wall busted. When I replaced that, I wondered if the pipes inside the wall would burst. Maybe they did, because soon both my showers started leaking, meaning I had to tear into two walls in order to replace the pipes. My handyman took months before finishing the re-tiling. That meant I kept having to shower with a plastic tarp that would billow out and engulf me. Sometimes I'd cry while showering—no more boyfriend to shower with, just this plastic tarp.

But the loss of my relationship meant I began to come out to more and more people, because I needed friends.

So I called William first. William was a gay church member who was one of the volunteers who helped with the youth. We arranged to meet at his house and walk down to a nice outdoor café in his neighborhood. As we walked, I began to tell him my story. I told him I needed friends and support.

William was a great listener. He also asked questions. The one that stuck with me was "What took you so long?"

A few years later I asked two close college friends, both also gay and out, why they had been surprised when I came out to them, because hardly anyone else among my old friends had been surprised.

Tom answered for them both. "You were always so self-actualized," he said. "I assumed you would have dealt with it by then, so I took you at your word that you were not gay."

After William, I came out to other gay men at church, despite Harry's warning. By the summer of 2004 a small group of us had begun to form a tight social circle. We would often go to lunch after worship on Sundays and out for drinks after choir rehearsal on Wednesday nights.

Logan and Brandon owned a jewelry store and lived in Plano. They were, in many ways, your typical suburban couple.

Daniel lived right in the middle of the "gayborhood." His house was the closest to the intersection of Throckmorton and Cedar Springs, the heart of the gay district. Daniel was a disciplined and restrained person, loyal and hardworking.

One day they all arranged to give me my first tour of Dallas' gayborhood. *Here's the underwear store. There's the coffee shop. Here's the gay bookstore. Aren't these greeting cards hilarious? There's the leather store. Here's the leather bar. Don't you want to go inside and dance on the box? Here's the cowboy bar. This other bar is good for sitting on the balcony and watching people walk by. There's the lesbian bar. Here's where everyone has brunch. This is the dance club, but it's being remodeled and won't open until the end of the year.*

I began to embrace this new identity. I still didn't go out to the clubs on my own; I was afraid of being outed and losing my job. So I began to rent gay films at Blockbuster. Even that made me nervous. What if someone saw?

I learned a few things from renting gay films. Just because

a French film had a sexy cover didn't mean anything. Likely someone was going to die, and the film wouldn't be sexy at all; it would just make me more depressed. Most American gay films, at least in that period, were pretty dorky. Older ones were often about AIDS—also not helpful for the depression. Latin American films could usually be counted on to be sexy.

And I began reading gay books. When one comes out, there is an entire culture to learn. Unlike other minorities where you grow up in the culture, most gay men grow up in isolation. So I was surprised and angry to learn that many key historical and literary figures were gay, like Alan Turing and Walt Whitman. How helpful it would have been to know in tenth grade.

Over the next year, I began to haunt the LGBT section of Half Price Books, devouring anthologies of gay literature, gay histories, social and cultural commentary, queer theory, and gay fiction. And being a philosopher, I also read Michel Foucault's three-volume *History of Sexuality*. Nothing like a little post-modern French philosophy to lift your spirits.

My sister began talking to me again late that spring, but it was nothing like the close relationship we'd had before the conversation behind the outlet mall. We largely avoided talking about anything having to do with my life. Even after she learned of the breakup, she didn't want to talk about it. We mainly talked about Mom's upcoming marriage.

Mom had moved to Oklahoma City a few years before. She'd finally become tired of the limitations of life in our small hometown and the lack of eligible men to date. She joined the First Baptist Church of Oklahoma City before she even moved or found a job there. For months she drove six hours round trip to attend church at a congregation which believed in female equality. Eventually she got a job in the city and moved there, and she met Harold shortly after.

Harold was new to town as well, having recently moved from Denver. He was getting a divorce. Harold worked as an auditor at the U.S. Department of Housing and Urban Development's Oklahoma City office. He was a quiet, gentle man who also enjoyed biking, running, and fishing. They met at church and started dating quickly thereafter.

I was so happy for Mom. Finally, after all these years, she had someone to do things with. She started biking, traveling, and generally being more physically active. She lost weight and radiated joy.

The afternoon before the wedding, I had to get away from everyone for a while, the energy of faking happiness having taken its toll. So I drove to Lake Hefner, where I sat by the water and cried, getting it out of my system.

I had decided after things went south with John, that the time to tell Mom was approaching. But I wanted to wait until after her wedding; I didn't want to risk spoiling her happiness. *Would my mother abandon me like my sister had? Would I be left alone in the world?*

I was not performing the wedding ceremony; a chaplain friend of Mom's was. But I was giving a blessing. The night before the wedding, Mom had a barbecue so we could meet Harold's family and vice versa. That family party was the first time I had seen my sister since she abandoned me behind the outlet mall. We were pretty good at faking politeness in front of everyone else. Mom later said she knew we were fighting, but didn't know what it was about.

That weekend I had hoped to see John and fix our relationship, but that meeting didn't happen. He didn't respond to any of my overtures. Instead, I was at this celebration while in the midst of a secret depression. I'm glad we white southerners are skilled at repressing our emotions.

The wedding was a nice event in Mom's backyard with around forty guests. She had spent months getting her garden to look just right. She was beaming.

On May 17 of that year, the Massachusetts Supreme Court legalized marriage between same-sex couples.

10

"Scott, why should that matter?"

I spent two days on the beach near Galveston with two of my other youth minister colleagues. While I was there, I bought a silly straw cowboy hat I decided to wear a few weeks later on the first day of youth camp. That year, I was in charge of the morning program we called "Come Alive." I was supposed to wake everyone up, get everyone excited, and set the mood and theme for the day. A great assignment for someone who was secretly depressed. One of the adult women from Royal Lane told me, "You need to take that hat off. It looks silly and you look gay. And if that is the look you are going for, then we need to have a talk." I put the hat away.

In June, still depressed, I attended our denomination's annual gathering in Birmingham, Alabama. As I did every year, I bought a bunch of books and went back to the hotel room to peruse them. I began reading Jurgen Moltmann's *In the End —The Beginning: The Life of Hope*. Moltmann is one of the most prominent living theologians, and I had not read any of his books before. Unlike most of them, this one was thin, so I was hoping it would be an easy read, nothing more than a quick introduction to his theology.

Sitting on my hotel bed, I started perusing the introduction, and I pretty much didn't put the book down until I had finished it two days later. I didn't attend any workshops or breakout sessions during the conference; I spent almost the entire time reading that book. Moltmann's message about resurrection was what I needed at that moment.

The theme of the book is that the central tenet of the Christian faith—the meaning of the resurrection—is that with every end there is a new beginning. Ours is a faith of hope, a faith that looks to the future. Moltmann emphasized that in every moment there are an indefinite number of possible futures, so after a disruption or a catastrophe in our lives, we should get up again. He used the line "Christians are the eternal beginners."

I was determined to overcome my depression and begin again. I could have retreated back into the closet, thinking that my exploration of a same-sex relationship had been a failure. But the few times John and I had been together had revealed truths about myself. I was indeed attracted to men. I found physical and emotional fulfillment with a man. For a few weeks in the spring, I had been happier than at any other point in my life.

But right then, that summer, life really sucked.

I finally heard from John at the end of June. He wrote a letter in which he detailed what happened from his perspective—I had fucked it up, being too pushy and needy.

I hadn't heard from Sarah and Lucas in months.

Over the Fourth of July weekend, I hung out with an old college friend who was bisexual. I hoped that maybe something might come of that. But he wasn't interested. I left early and drove home.

I finally tried to talk to my sister again about my being gay and about my relationship ending. She said, "I love you, but I can't have this in my life."

After a pause, I responded, "Those two things don't go together, and you need to realize that."

So, one day in July I was mowing the lawn and dripping with sweat. As I marched up and down the yard, I kept mulling over my situation. I wanted to live more fully into my identity as a gay man and have more experiences. But my relationship had ended and I was still depressed. I was fashioning a social and support group, which was helping. I was working hard on getting well, despite the unremitting sadness that struck me at times. I was determined to rise from this catastrophe and begin again.

But what if I did all the difficult work of getting well from this depression and then lost my family, or my job, or both? That would send me spiraling back into depression. I realized right then, dripping with sweat on a hot summer day, that it would be better to get it all over with at once. *If life is going to suck,* I thought, *let's just get the worst over with and then figure out how to start over again.* I decided that I'd tell Ray and my Mom that very week. *One week,* I thought, *and done.*

That afternoon Ray, Harry, and I were sitting in Ray's office planning the week's worship service, when at a break in the conversation, I simply said, "Ray, I'm gay."

Ray kept his composure, but I could tell he was stunned, probably more by the surprise of me bringing it up in that moment than by the actual news. What sticks with me is how little he reacted in that moment. He had an abnormal ability to keep calm. Harry, however, looked alarmed. I noticed he was sweating.

It shocks me how little I remember of that scene in Ray's office. I vividly remember the looks on their faces, but their words escape me. He didn't fire me right then. That seemed to be the most important thing at the time.

The conversation that day wasn't long. Ray expressed encouragement for me personally, but he sounded the note of caution. He said he was worried about the impact on the congregation. He told me he wanted time to think, and asked me not to tell anyone else while he was deciding how to respond. I told him I planned to tell my mother and stepfather that week.

Reflecting on the moment days later, something bothered me—Ray never asked my story. Alone among all the people I ever came out to, Ray never asked about how I had wrestled with that decision or any other personal details. I would have like my friend and respected mentor to ask.

Later, secluded in his office, Harry told me he wished I had warned him. "You promised me that," he said, clearly disappointed and angry.

"I know. I'm sorry about that," I said. "But I decided this morning that I simply had to do it. I knew you'd try to dissuade me if I told you ahead of time." I knew I'd hurt my friend, but hoped he'd forgive me.

"You are correct. I think it was a mistake to tell Ray."

I explained to him the decision I had made that morning while mowing the lawn.

"I want to tell Mom on Friday," I said. "Will you drive with me to Oklahoma City and back? I know the drive's six hours round trip, but I don't want to go alone."

"Yes, Scott. I can do that for you," Harry said. I was relieved that my promise-breaking had not shattered our friendship.

Harry asked, "How do you think your mother will respond?"

"When I was in eighth grade she told me that if I was gay she would kill herself," I said with a smirk.

"She really said that? You never told me that before." Harry was wide-eyed.

"Yeah. So I can imagine a whole range of possible responses."

"Like what?" he asked.

"At best, I think she'll throw some sort of fit, crying and wailing. At worst she could walk down the hall to her bedroom, take her handgun out of her nightstand, and shoot herself."

"You're joking, right?" he asked. "I can't imagine your mother doing that."

"No, I'm not joking." And I wasn't. I was trying to be matter-of-fact and realistic, planning for all possibilities, but also not letting those outcomes frighten me away from being honest.

"I don't think that's what she'll do," I said, shrugging my shoulders, "but it is within the realm of possibility."

Harry looked tenderly at me, "I think you can set yourself at ease that she won't shoot herself with a handgun."

I smirked again. "I honestly don't know how she'll react, but I don't think she'll take it well. Remember, I thought Erin would be okay, and that was a disaster."

"Yeah, that was," he agreed.

That afternoon I called Mom and lied, telling her that Harry and I were going to be in Oklahoma City on Friday for a work thing and asking if I could stop by. She said she'd expect me after work on Friday.

She was dressed in a nice business suit when I arrived at her house. Harry had dropped me off and driven away to kill time, telling me to call when I wanted to be picked up.

I told Mom and Harold that we needed to talk. He offered to leave us alone, but I invited him to stay. We sat in the living room instead of the den. Wood floors, yellow walls, lace curtains, and that pale floral pattern on the sofa. This was the same sofa we'd been sitting on years before when Mom told me of the revelation she'd had before I was born that I was special and that God would use me to do great work.

Mom sat down next to me, he hands clasped in her lap. Harold sat in the green armchair beside us, the one he used for reading and napping in the afternoon.

And so I began. I took a deep breath, but I could hardly get the words out before the tears welled up. My mother reached over and held my hand. When I said I was gay, she didn't remove her hand, didn't shudder, didn't recoil, didn't go for her handgun.

"Oh Scotty," she said. "I still love you."

Harold reached over and put his hand on my knee. "Scott, why should that matter?" he said. "I love you like my own son. This doesn't change anything."

I began to cry even more, as decades of pain and secrecy lifted suddenly from me. My mother and I were close, but there had always been some tension between us. We'd look forward to spending time together, yet we often began arguing within the first few minutes of a visit. In the months after I came out to her I realized how often in the past my fear of rejection had gotten in the way of our relationship.

Mom and Harold listened as I told them the story, including everything about John and our breakup.

"This explains what I've been sensing in recent months," Mom said, sounding relieved. "It seemed that you were emotionally distant, even at our wedding. I thought it was because I was getting remarried."

I felt guilty for that. I had tried my best to hide my depression during the wedding, obviously unsuccessfully.

"That weekend was the first time I was in Oklahoma City and wasn't going to see John," I told them. "That day before you got married, I drove over to Lake Hefner to sit beside the water and just collect myself, because I knew I couldn't be emotional at your wedding."

She sighed. "You know, when you called the other day, I decided that you were coming to tell me that you were severely depressed and needed my help in finding treatment."

I guess I hadn't been very successful at hiding my emotions.

She continued. "That's actually why I stayed dressed up in my work clothes, in case we needed to go to the hospital. In many ways, what you've told me is such a relief compared to what I expected." Hearing that was quite a surprise and a relief to me as well.

She was shocked when I told her about Erin. "I'm disappointed. You would never treat your sister that way."

Near the close of the conversation, Mom said that she would still need some time to process everything and would also need help understanding a few things. "I'm going to call my chaplain friend and talk to her about everything," she said.

"That's a good idea," I said.

"I can't help it," she said. "I'm worried about you. Worried that something will happen with your job, though I am convinced that God will open another door. I'm also afraid you could get beaten up." Then she looked down. "Or that you could get sick."

I knew she meant AIDS. "Mom, both of those things are unlikely," I said. "First, I'm very cautious, so it's unlikely I'm going to get beat up. Second, I'm not going to be stupid. I'm going to take precautions and be safe. Okay?"

She hugged me, and we stood there holding each other for a moment. She cried as she told me she loved me.

On the way home, Harry said, "See, she didn't kill herself."

11

We bathed ourselves in the cool waters.

Mom called a week or so later. In the midst of our conversation she asked, "What are you attracted to in other men?"

I sputtered and then managed to say, "Thank you for your interest, Mom, but I really don't think I want to discuss that with my mother." I appreciated that she was at least trying, but there is such a thing as trying too hard.

Mom had talked with her chaplain friend.

"She told me there was something I needed to read. She sent it to me and I printed it off. It is called 'The Letter to Louise.' It was written by an elderly Southern Baptist minister who studied the issue of homosexuality and changed his mind. The letter is written to a friend of his with a gay brother encouraging her to support her brother."

"Mom, yes, I know 'The Letter to Louise,'" I said, almost laughing. "Bruce Lowe, the author, is a member of Royal Lane."

"Oh, my," she exclaimed. "Are you serious?"

I first met Bruce and his wife, Anna Marie, before I moved to Dallas. We met at the General Assembly in Atlanta, Georgia, when the Cooperative Baptist Fellowship voted on the Coordinating Council's anti-gay policy. Bruce attended the meeting in order to support the full inclusion of gay people. I was moved to admiration seeing this frail, white-haired man in his late eighties standing on the side of LGBT rights. Little did I know that within a few years I would be serving as associate pastor in the church where Bruce and Anna Marie were members.

Bruce was a veteran of civil rights battles. In the 1960s, he was fired by the church he pastored when he preached in support of the full inclusion of African-Americans. He got a job with the Justice Department and traveled the South checking on hospitals to make sure that they were fully integrated and were serving their African-American patients equally.

When he was eighty years old, his friend Louise came to him worried about her gay brother. She wanted to know if he would go to hell. Bruce grimaced and said that was his understanding of the Bible. Anna Marie objected. She said that couldn't be true. Bruce listened to his wife and realized that he had never studied the issue and that it was wrong of him to comment since he had never looked carefully at the topic.

In the course of the next few months, he read forty books on homosexuality. He read theology, biblical commentary, sociology, scientific studies, and more, representing various viewpoints. At the conclusion of his study, he realized that he had spoken from ignorance. He wrote that he now deplored his earlier ignorance, which had resulted in prejudice.

Once informed, he completely changed his position on the topic and wrote "The Letter to Louise" summarizing what he had learned. He then became an advocate for LGBT equality, hosting a website godmademegay.com where he shared his story and the letter. He also corresponded with people who wrote to him, answering their questions and providing pastoral support. Over the years he helped many families accept their gay children and helped many LGBT persons reconcile their identity and their faith.

The presence of Bruce and Anna Marie Lowe at Royal Lane Baptist Church was one reason I believed the congregation could handle my coming out. I knew he would support me, and I thought only a callous person could know Bruce and not be persuaded by him.

Ray reacted the next week. He told me he had been shocked by my news and didn't know initially how to respond. He wanted the three of us to meet and talk about how to proceed.

So, Harry, Ray, and I gathered in his office again. Clearly they had talked ahead of time. They asked me not to tell any more people and to be less open about my sexuality for a few months because they felt like "the dam was about to break," as Harry put it. They recommended that I go to counseling to deal with all the changes and with my depression. At the conclusion of the meeting, they asked me to write out what we had agreed to and sign it. I said I would.

But that evening, when I was finally home alone and had time to reflect on the conversation, I decided I couldn't do it. Writing those things out would feel like a breach of my integrity. I wouldn't be happy with myself, and I'd be constantly second-guessing everything I said and did. I knew that if I signed the document, I would come to resent them.

Resigning appeared to be the only option before me. I was angry that my friends didn't have the guts to back me and trust the church to handle this well.

In the midst of all my personal crises, my professional responsibilities continued. That weekend I was off with the youth on a mission trip to south Texas, so I had a reprieve in which to think and to decide. I suppose most of the youth and adults I worked with could tell I wasn't as energetic and enthusiastic as I normally was, but I am certain that most had no idea what was going on.

For our mission trip that year, we were in the appropriately named Mission, Texas, in the border region along the Rio Grande that Texans call The Valley. This region has a noticeable wealth inequality. There are signs of economic development and vitality, much of it rooted in agriculture. But the Valley is also home to some of the worst poverty in the United States. We were remodeling family homes in the *colonias*, unincor- porated housing developments for migrant workers and new immigrants.

In the rare quiet moments during the trip, I reflected on the conversation with Ray and Harry. In the evenings I tried to steal away to an orchard at the campground where we stayed, walking along the row of orange trees and taking in their scent as I meditated upon my predicament.

Resignation really did seem to be the only option. On the

practical level, I wondered what I would do to earn a living. But what really concerned me was the question of identity— *if I was no longer a minister, then who was I?* My effort since the previous fall to fulfill both callings—Christian ministry and being an out gay man—seemed to be failing.

In this moment of existential crisis, I punted. When I returned from the mission trip to south Texas, I avoided following up on the conversation with Ray and Harry. Because summer was my busy season with all my youth out of school and the college students home, avoidance was easy. I decided that as long as I did my job and worked hard, I could avoid any conflict.

I had never seen a therapist before and was curious and excited about the novelty of the experience before the first visit. I was also nervous, of course. The appointment was early on a Wednesday morning, at an address about six miles south of my house just off of the Central Expressway, so I got to experience the joys of the Dallas morning commute. The office was in a pink tower. A Thai restaurant occupied the first floor. I thought I might return for lunch sometime, but I never did.

I rode the elevator to the fifth floor and located the office. The entry door led to a small waiting room with the typical array of fake plants, old magazines, and bad art on the walls. There was no reception desk or other person sitting in the waiting room. I was unsure of the procedure, so I simply sat down to wait. Eventually, an inner door opened and a kind-looking, white-haired man introduced himself as Dr. Williams and invited me into his office.

Since Ray had made the referral, Dr. Williams knew some of the basics, but of course he wanted to hear everything from my perspective. That first session was a pretty basic recounting of the story of my coming out, the breakup with John, and my struggle with what to do about my job. I also said that we should probably talk some about the death of my father, since I'd never had any therapy for that and probably should have. At the close of the session, a few tissues were piled beside me on the couch. I carried them to the waste bin.

We talked about my father's death in the third session. At the end, the pile of tissues beside me on the couch was quite large. Dr. Williams told me to not avoid thoughts about John when they came to me, but that I should use them for self-analysis. Well, that was no fun.

What I eventually figured out wasn't rocket science—I had fallen for John too quickly and the burden of my own issues and expectations was probably too much for him. I needed to develop my own emotional strength and quit focusing on John's actions. Realizing you need to fix yourself isn't an enjoyable thing to learn. How much easier it is to complain about someone else.

Dr. Williams told me that any happiness the winter before had been generated by me, not by John. Hearing that was like getting slapped upside the head, but in a good way.

Harry confronted me in early August. He pulled me into the sanctuary and insisted on talking through all the issues. He said I owed them a response; I needed to follow through on what I had said I would do back in July. The way he painted the picture, I would be unable to continue working at Royal Lane if I didn't craft a statement and sign it. Harry said that the congregation wasn't ready for me to be an out gay minister, and that he and Ray weren't ready to lead that charge. I responded that I didn't want to continue hiding much longer. "Don't ask, don't tell" wasn't going to work for me.

Hiding and passing were already harming my personal integrity. One day I was at a lunch meeting with a church member in order to discuss some Christian education issues when she asked, "Scott, are you gay?"

"No," I lied, fearing for my job. I later learned, from her kind support, that she would have been an ally, but I didn't know that then.

The morning after the confrontation with Harry, I went into work prepared to meet with Ray and offer my resignation. But my conversation with Ray went completely differently than the conversation with Harry the day before. Ray thought I could continue, that I was doing the job well, and that the therapy should help. We'd found a middle way. I wouldn't have to pledge in writing to their terms, but I agreed to live within them for the time being while I continued to explore my identity privately. This agreement would also be a reprieve, giving me time to consider my career options and to make plans instead of offering a resignation without any idea of where my next paycheck and health care would come from or whether I'd be able to fulfill my lifelong sense of call to Christian ministry.

The next week I was off to Georgia with two of the young adults from church and Mary Lou, who was sixty-four years old and an experienced hiker. She would be our guide on our excursion along the southern end of the Appalachian Trail. Our rental van had a DVD player and everyone else watched movies as I drove the long hours through Louisiana, Mississippi, and Alabama.

The air in the mountains was clear and crisp instead of the hazy, polluted sky we'd been enduring in Dallas. Our small group exchanged the hot summer of the city for pleasant days and cool nights in the mountains.

Hiking and camping was a new experience for me, and I was exhilarated. My soul felt refreshed, though trudging up and down the mountains was awfully painful on my feet and carrying the heavy pack hurt my shoulders. One day I felt so exhausted I seriously considered lying down and going to sleep in the middle of the trail. I learned that in the midst of a grueling hike, we'd round a corner and find sublime beauty. Reaching these paradises took exhausting work. There seemed to be a spiritual lesson there.

One night we camped at Long Creek Falls, a place you can only reach by hiking. It looked like something out of a movie set: tall pine trees, rhododendron trees down low, a bed of pine needles (which made for nice sleeping), and an incredible cascading falls. I rested my weary feet in a soft bed of moss. We bathed ourselves in the cool waters.

That night it rained, and Eden turned miserable. Inside our leaky tent, I curled into a fetal position to avoid the drip near my head and the puddle forming near my feet.

On the final day, as we descended Mt. Springer approaching Amicalola Falls State Park, the hike was gentle and the weather was perfectly pleasant. The sun shone brightly, filtering through the trees like "God-light" on cheesy calendars. Along one stretch I marveled at intricate cobwebs that glistened beside the trail and became convinced that the spiders in that section of Georgia were some of the most elaborate and interesting architects in the world.

That evening, off the trail, we stuffed ourselves on chicken fried steaks and enjoyed long, warm showers and sleeping in beds.

12

I still had a lot to learn.

This really could be me, I thought as I watched all the same-sex couples pushing babies in strollers. I was in Chicago on vacation and a friend took me to the farmer's market in Andersonville, which was then becoming the neighborhood for lesbian and gay families with kids.

We also went to Boystown, one of the truly great gayborhoods. The street is aglow with neon lights, and the shop windows entice with sexy underwear in bright colors and sex toys best left to the imagination. The street is vibrant and fun, filled with all kinds of attractive men. I felt like I'd arrived at a buffet.

I was enjoying finally noticing men sexually. For decades, any time something about a guy attracted me I looked away and put the thought aside. Finally I was allowing myself to keep looking. And I discovered how infinitely attractive men are. This one has great hair. That one is muscular. This one is thin and fit and looks great in tight clothes. That one is burly and hot. A smorgasbord of different types of bodies, styles, and personalities.

We went to Sidetracks, the great video bar, where I thrilled to the crowd of mostly young, well-dressed, good-looking gay men singing along to film clips from Broadway shows. An ecstasy arose within me from being in a crowded room filled with other gay men. After all the loneliness and isolation of the previous months, this moment felt like heaven.

Toward the end of the evening a cute guy, a sommelier who had introduced himself to us earlier in the night, sat down at the bar beside me and kissed me. He then kept kissing me and clearly would have been interested in more, except that my inexperience with such things got in the way.

Bruce Lowe's "The Letter to Louise" had addressed many of my mother's scriptural and theological questions. It had also given her some sense that elderly Southern Baptists (like Pappoo, maybe) could be pro-gay. But much about gay life eluded her understanding. She was most familiar with the stereotypes common in the media, which made her uncomfortable. What she saw on television wasn't exactly what she wanted for her son. I decided now was the time for her to meet more gay people.

She and Harold came to Dallas for a visit. We did our normal shopping, sightseeing, and bike riding along the trail from my neighborhood down to White Rock Lake (a favorite of theirs whenever they visited). But this time I also planned a party for Mom and Harold to meet more gay people.

Brandon and Logan offered to host at their home in Plano. The location alone would send a signal, for Plano is one of the most boring stretches of suburb in the country. They invited the other gay men and women from church to the party.

Brandon emailed all of them letting them know the purpose of the event—Scott's parents needed to meet gay people in order to be more at ease about Scott's coming out. Everyone was excited to participate.

When we arrived at their house, Logan, who's over six feet tall, handsome, with dark hair and a rich Southern accent, greeted Mom with a big hug, shook Harold's hand, then took them on a tour of their house. He even showed them the bedroom. Mom later went on about how nice the house was and how gracious Logan was.

Brandon, who had an even richer Southern accent and was blonde, was in the kitchen finishing up the potato soup he had cooked for the event. He and Mom chatted about cooking. "The kitchen is my domain," Brandon said. "Logan is not allowed in it." Mom identified and laughed.

Other friends began to arrive, and the conversation in the living room turned to military service, as Harold is a Vietnam vet and some of the other guys were veterans as well. They also spoke of football. Later we joked that the conversation topics had remained rather butch and that no one had talked about how they enjoyed the tight-fitting football uniforms.

Yes, everyone was on their best, heteronormative behavior. Not the best example of queer liberation, but the event worked. As we drove back to my house, Mom said, "Thank you for arranging that. I really needed to meet other gay people and see that you had a support group. I really liked all of them. Please let them know how much that meant to me."

I emailed the group the next day, "Mission accomplished," and they were all happy to have helped achieve the desired result.

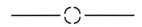

A church member called to say she had a student, a gay man, whom she wanted me to meet. I was not out to this church member, but the way that the conversation was going, I wasn't sure whether she wanted me to meet the young man for professional, pastoral reasons or for personal reasons, either friendship or a setup for a date. So, I decided to take a risk and directly ask her.

"Are you wanting me to meet him for pastoral care? Or do you think we should be friends? Or are you setting us up on a date?"

She giggled. "Any," she said. "Or all three."

So much for the idea that I was successfully passing at church.

She introduced us the next day. I had arrived at her house first, so when the door opened and Martin walked in, I was taken by his beauty—lovely blonde hair that I wanted to run my fingers through, bright, sparkling blue eyes that one could linger watching, full, red lips I was already imagining kissing, and a smile to die for. In every way he seemed like a sweet, gentle, nice guy.

Martin was only 22 and just out of college. He coached at a cheerleading school. He was from a small Texas town and had been out since he was 15. He had recently ended a four-year relationship with a man twenty years older.

We soon arranged our first date.

"I don't know how to date," I said to Matt Cox, having called to talk about this new possibility.

"You're thinking too much," Matt said with a sigh. "Just relax and enjoy yourself."

"But I didn't think last time at all," I said with some frustration, hoping for better advice. "I did relax and enjoy myself with John. I let myself fall in love quickly and then it was so painful."

"Well, don't do that, either," he said with a gentle laugh.

Still exasperated, I said, "But, see, I don't know what to do. How do I relax and enjoy myself and not get hurt again?"

"There is no guarantee," Matt said. "Just don't fall so quickly. But still have fun. If you're on your guard too much then it won't be fun, and the relationship won't have any chance of working."

"This is all so complicated," I said, having gained no helpful information.

For the date, I was able to get free symphony tickets from a friend. Martin had never been to the symphony before, but said he was interested. The schedule would be tight. He would get off work in barely enough time for us to grab a quick dinner before the concert began. The plan was for him to come to my house straight from work and get ready there. When I opened the door, he was in tight-fitting workout clothes that showed off his physique. He was gorgeous.

We had that quick dinner, enjoyed the symphony (Verdi's *Requiem*), and went for dessert afterwards at Café Brazil. Then we came back to my house and played *Super Mario Brothers 3* on my old Nintendo for two hours.

Over the course of the next month, we hung out about once a week. We went to the movies. I took him soup when he was sick. He visited church and had lunch with my friends.

A month after that first date, I planned a romantic evening with an expensive dinner at a French restaurant. I had never ordered a bottle of wine before, but Martin took charge and picked it out. He knew a lot about food and helped direct me to my choices. That dinner cost me $150, which was way more than I'd ever spent on dinner before.

We were sitting on the restaurant's patio, enjoying the warm November night, and the conversation got more personal than our conversations of the past month. I expressed my desire to share more with him and get to know him better. He shared more about himself and his relationship and the pain over his breakup. I shared about mine. He talked about what he was looking for in a relationship. I was hopeful that things were going to develop.

That night when we returned to my house and were standing in the living room, I was hoping for a first kiss, but before I could make any move in that direction, Martin said a hasty goodbye, gave me his normal hug, and left.

The bedside lamp in my bedroom was burning, as I had turned it on earlier that evening imagining the possibilities when we came home from dinner. I walked into the bedroom, turned off the lamp, and lay down on the bed feeling confused. After a month, no goodnight kiss. We hadn't even held hands. Everything seemed to be going well, but surely the lack of any romantic touch was a sign.

And it was. The next night he called to say he only wanted to be friends.

Besides the annual gay pride festival and parade, the other big night in the gayborhood in Dallas was the Halloween Block Party. Cedar Springs was closed to vehicular traffic while the well-costumed people of Dallas paraded up and down the street to wild applause. Before dark, it was a family-friendly event. After dark, not so much. For every elaborate, unique, and creative costume, other people were clothed in racy costumes or simply scantily clad. I vividly remember two young gay guys who walked hand-in-hand down the street wearing nothing but their tight bikini briefs and angel wings, one in black, the other in white.

I went with friends from church. We sat out on Daniel's deck, where we could see the parade as it passed the intersection of Throckmorton and Cedar Springs. I was dressed in a maroon leisure suit and a yellow silk shirt, all of which I had picked up in a thrift shop once for a youth group event. Logan unbuttoned the top button of my silk shirt and said, "You need to be sexier." I still had a lot to learn.

I also decided, after the work crisis of the previous summer, to reassert my own power over my coming-out process. I shared my story with close friends who lived other places than Dallas. So I began to live two different lives that fall. One life as an out gay man, primarily with people who lived elsewhere. And another, closeted life among those people I worked with and lived near. Paradoxically, my close friends who lived in Dallas, who I spent time with regularly, did not yet know. In that way I was trying to find the middle ground in my agreement with Ray and Harry.

I had begun blogging back in April. One of the other young guys at Royal Lane encouraged me to start. He had read some of my writing and thought I'd be good at this new medium. I began in April, about the time my relationship with John was falling apart.

The name of my blog was "MyQuest," with the subtitle "My thoughts on life's journey." For years, my Wednesday night youth group had been called "TheQuest," so the idea behind the title was that the blog would be a place to share my personal perspective on the adventure of faith.

My original motive in writing, however, was mostly political. Since high school I had been a Republican, and I had even voted for George W. Bush in the 2000 election. But I was very discouraged by the war in Iraq and the various policies created after September 11, 2001. As with many moderate, progressive, and old-school Republicans, by 2004, I was quite disenchanted. I wanted to share my views, and this new blogging thing seemed like the perfect way to do that. So, my first post was entitled "A Former Republican Against Bush."

Because of the blog, I developed new friendships online with other progressive, social justice-inclined Christians. A group of people living in Oklahoma City became my closest blogging friends. We had real-world ties; many of us shared friends in common and some of us had attended OBU. A few were even liberal (or getting there) Baptist ministers.

We soon learned that most of the people in the blog circle shared a fondness for the essays and poetry of Wendell Berry, so we began to call ourselves "The Wendell Berry Society of Greater Oklahoma City" (my living in Dallas vastly expanding the idea of "Greater Oklahoma City"). The commitment to Berry became quite real when one couple, the O'Briens, followed Berry's ideals to the point of selling their home in Oklahoma City and building a farmhouse almost an hour outside of the city where they began trying to raise much of their own food. In later years our group would gather at the farm and hang out late into the night drinking craft beers while discussing poetry, the existence of God, and the latest ordeals in raising chickens.

Soon I was out to all these blogging friends, which increased the fun of my visits back to Oklahoma. It also made blogging more interesting, as my new friends learned to read between the lines of what I was sharing publicly. I began to send subtle messages to them through the blog. I think my dual life increased my blog's readership for that period, because it introduced a level of suspense—would I say something, or would someone else write something that outed me?

Oklahoma City was quickly becoming the place where I could be more fully myself. Which is ironic, because lots of closeted gay Oklahomans enjoy visiting Dallas, where they are able to be out.

One day in therapy, Dr. Williams told me I had cast John as a character in a fantasy that, at least at first, he had somewhat fulfilled. I became addicted to the projection. So ever since John quit living up to it, I had been in withdrawal.

I realized how many times over the years, from high school on, in one experience after another, I had longed for some guy to seduce me and awaken my sexuality. I had always been too scared to make the move myself. Finally, with John, I had made it happen. I had taken the initiative and been the agent, which was a good thing. But I had also placed the burden of all those years of fantasies onto John, the one person who I knew was into me.

The projection had worked at first. I had gotten my fantasy, my sexuality had been awakened, and a new world had opened to me. John-the-projection had become, even after the breakup, the storehouse of all those decades of fantasies, repressions, and desires, plus my newfound liberation and joy. But John wasn't a fantasy. He was an actual person, and this had all been too much for him.

Damn right, I missed him. John-the-projection was a deep part of my own psyche.

What Dr. Williams helped me realize that autumn was that I'd already experienced the fantasy, and the fantasy was wonderful. But I didn't need it any longer. I needed to move on and claim all of that as part of my own identity, rather than projecting it onto other guys. I also needed to be more easygoing and relaxed in my relationships, which required that I become more comfortable in my sexual identity and freer in my sexuality.

That week I wrote John a letter of apology. Did I harbor secret desires that he would forgive me and send a similar letter? Oh, sure, I did. I am human, after all. But he never replied, and that was okay.

13

"Is Scotty gay?"

My uncle Harley and his new girlfriend, Debra, offered to host the family Thanksgiving that year. Debra is from Taiwan, a widow and the mother of three kids. She lived in a big suburban home in southwest Oklahoma City that was filled with lighted glass display cases exhibiting her collection of crystal. She was a beautician who had built her own small business empire.

Thanksgiving has always been my favorite holiday. Christmas is complicated with all the parties, gifts, and heightened expectations. Thanksgiving is simple: cooking, eating, watching football, napping, and later maybe playing games or going to a movie.

I also feel pride that the holiday is part of our family's heritage. According to the genealogical work that my Mom's cousin Marcia did in the 1980s, eight of my ancestors sailed to America on the *Mayflower*. One of those, Elizabeth Tilley Howland, gave advice to her descendants which I took to heart as an adolescent: *It is my Will & Charge to all my Children that they walk in the Fear of the Lord, and in Love and peace towards each other.*

Mom and I went over to Debra and Harley's house a little early to help get things ready. I ended up in the kitchen drinking wine and assisting occasionally. That's where I met Debra's son, Christopher, who was doing a lot of the cooking. He told me he was completing a Women's Studies degree at the University of Oklahoma. He was very fit and had a roguish smile.

My gay-dar was pinging, so I began the subtle, coded conversation to determine if the pings were accurate. Soon, Chris's "friend," David, arrived. At that, even Mom gave me a knowing look.

By dinnertime, all of my family had arrived, and so had Debra's next-door neighbors—a middle-aged gay couple. Soon I was sitting at the table with the two gay couples, and we were having a pretty open chat. I was really enjoying myself.

This experience taught me who among my extended family were more perceptive than others. Pappoo, for instance, gave no evidence of having noticed that all these men were gay.

Mom and Harold left shortly after dinner. I wasn't ready to leave, so my aunt Karen offered to take me back to Mom's house later on. But by the time she was ready to go, I'd arranged to go out to some clubs with Chris and David. They said they would drop me off at Mom's later that night. Karen said okay, but I noticed that she seemed hesitant. Karen was astute enough to know Chris and David were gay, and I could tell that she was, in that moment, wondering about me. Karen and I had always had a good relationship. She was an elementary school art teacher, and when I was a kid she'd always have some art project for us to work on together. I felt that surely Karen wouldn't judge me, but in the moment I was too excited to worry about what her reaction might be.

Chris and David took me out for my first visit to Oklahoma

City's gay strip, which wasn't a whole gayborhood like Cedar Springs in Dallas or Boystown in Chicago. There were no coffee shops, bookstores, or other shops that indicated day-time energy and life. Nor was it a residential area for gays. The Strip in Oklahoma City was a somewhat sparse grouping of old buildings situated along a couple blocks of Northwest 39th Street. You could hear the big trucks blow by on I-44, which bordered the neighborhood to the north. A run-down apart-ment complex occupied one side of the street. I was warned to stay away from it and also the car wash at the other end where the hustlers supposedly hung out.

The landmark of The Strip was, and remains, the Habana Inn. The hotel housed three gay bars and a decent restaurant. I would come to learn that the Habana was infamous in gay circles as a hook-up spot. An entertaining (though somewhat creepy) activity was to walk around the hotel and catch a glimpse of the activities, as many inhabitants would leave their room curtains open. The Habana is a relic of a different age, but one that hasn't completely dissipated in Oklahoma. Cruising spots like these are still a feature of the repressive life of clos-eted men. On weekends the Habana fills with men from rural areas—farmers, ranchers, and oil field workers —who can't live openly as gay men during the week.

Chris and David showed me all the bars, including The Park, where Chris worked some nights as a bartender, and they intro-duced me to friends and co-workers. I learned some useful things, too. They told me where to go for the strongest and cheapest drinks (Tramps). They told me the correct time to arrive at the dance club the Copa. Between 11 and 11:30 you could generally avoid waiting in line, but not be one of the early arrivers, which was vital because you wanted people to see you walk in. I also learned that Thanksgiving evening is one of the best times to go out to gay clubs, as people have spent all day with their families and want to get away and enjoy themselves for a while.

After the clubs closed at two, we went for breakfast at a diner. It was after three when Chris dropped me off at Mom's.

She was up waiting for me.

When I walked in, she was reading a book on the couch in the family room. She placed the book in her lap and looked up at me. She spoke softly, but with determination.

"You're coming in late," she said.

I closed the door behind me. "Yes, I went out with Chris and David." I crossed the room toward her. Her eyes appeared tired.

"Karen mentioned that they'd be bringing you home," she said. "I didn't realize it would be so late." I was physically tired and ready for bed, and also happy about all the new experiences. I really didn't want to have this conversation now.

"Well, we had a lot of fun." I sat down on the love seat across from her.

"Where did you go?" she asked.

"They took me out to the gay bars here in Oklahoma City and showed me around. We talked a lot. I told them my story."

"So, are they a couple?" I confirmed that they were. She smiled. "I thought so. I didn't expect all those gay people at our family Thanksgiving. It must have been nice for you."

I smiled back. "It was."

Then the smile left her face. "I hope Pappoo didn't figure everything out."

I sighed. "I'm sure he didn't." Then I changed the topic. "You know, you don't need to wait up for me. I am thirty years old."

Looking me directly in the eyes, she said, "Well, I was just worried and wanted to be sure you were safe."

I stood up. "I am. Thank you for being concerned. Now I'm going to bed. It's been a long day."

"You should probably wash the smoke smell off before you go to sleep." She opened the book again.

"Sure, I'll do that," I said, walking toward the hall. "Good night."

The next day after Karen departed to return home to Missouri, Mom said she had a story to tell me. While I was still asleep that morning, Karen had come into the kitchen where Mom was making coffee and said, "So, Scotty stayed out late with Chris and David last night."

Mom said she answered that I had. She then confided to me, "I knew Karen was fishing for more, but I was going to wait until she actually asked. When she figured out I wasn't going to say any more, she said, 'I think Chris and David are a gay couple.'"

"What did you say then?" I asked.

About to laugh, Mom said, "I responded, 'Yes, I think they are' and kept looking at the brewing coffee. Then, after another silence, Karen, who was also staring at the coffee pot by this time, asked, 'Did Scotty realize he was going out with a gay couple?'"

"I told her you did," Mom continued. "After that there was a long pause during which Karen awkwardly fumbled with her coffee mug. Then she finally asked her big question, 'Is Scotty gay?'"

"And what did you say to that?" I asked.

Mom laughed. "I simply said, 'Yes, he is,' and picked up the coffee pot and offered her some."

I'm sure Karen had an epiphany as to why I had enjoyed the movie *Troy* so much when she and I saw it together the previous spring.

After the events of Thanksgiving, most of my family knew I was gay. To my relief, there weren't any immediate, serious repercussions. Neither Harley nor Karen made a big deal out of it, and both of them expressed their support to Mom. Frank, the youngest sibling, seemed to be like Pappoo, completely oblivious.

Frank and I developed a close relationship when I moved to the metro area in 1992 to attend college at Oklahoma Baptist University. He had lived in the city for fifteen years at that point. Frank taught me how to drive in city traffic. "Speed up" was the basic tenet of his driving philosophy.

"If you want to change lanes, speed up," he'd say. "If you want to enter the highway, speed up. If you want to exit the highway, speed up. Basically, keep that one rule in mind. Speed up. And don't be around the State Capitol after dark. That's not a good area."

Frank was right wing in his political views. For Christmas in 1994 I gave him a nutcracker and labeled it "The Newt Cracker," named after Speaker of the House Newt Gingrich. Inside the box were a bunch of nuts and each was labeled with the name of a different Democrat I knew Frank despised. He loved it.

Even before my move to the political left, Frank's politics had always been to the right of mine, and years of Rush Limbaugh and Fox News hadn't helped. We had already had a series of loud arguments over the Iraq War.

Frank and I argued about politics, but he was always generous with his nieces and nephews, having never married or had kids of his own. He often gave us the best and most interesting Christmas and birthday gifts. In the early 1980s, for instance, when Cabbage Patch Dolls were the hot hard-to-find Christmas gift, he acquired two and gave them to my sister and cousin. The little girls were ecstatic.

When each of us started college, Frank opened American Express Card accounts in our names with the bills going to him. He told us he would cover about $25 in expenses a month as long as we stayed in college. He wanted to support us and also help us to build our credit. At the family party to celebrate the completion of my PhD, Frank said, "I didn't know you were going to spend nine years in college." Despite the remark, I knew he was proud to have helped.

Harley eventually told Frank I was gay, and Mom relayed the news to me. Frank wasn't happy about it. I think he was mostly disappointed. He had often talked about how he wanted me and my cousins to be successful people. I don't think Frank could imagine that I would lead a good and successful life as a gay man.

Only one time did Frank confront me with his negative views on homosexuality. We were once again at Harley and Debra's, this time for Chinese New Year. Frank was the first person seated at the dining room table when I walked in.

Without looking up at me, he said, "It's not right. Being gay."

Before I could respond, Harley walked in. His face red with anger, he marched over to where Frank was sitting.

"You're going to shut up right now," he said.

Frank started to reply, but Harley leaned closer and went on. "I said, you're going to shut up right now. If you don't, then you can leave this house and never come back again."

That shut Frank up.

As for Pappoo, Mom told me she had discussed the issue with Harley and Karen. They decided that telling him was a bad idea. He was a senior adult, they reasoned, and probably wouldn't understand. Plus, they thought, as long as no particular reason existed, like me having some guy I wanted to bring home for Christmas, it would be best to just leave well enough alone. I didn't share my family's opinion on the matter. But with everything else going on in my life, not riling them up seemed to be the smartest strategy, especially while they were being so supportive. I conceded to their decision that we would not tell Pappoo that I was gay.

14

"Imagine running into you here."

I was amused to see so many guys in their tight-fitting clothes shaking in the cold because they didn't want to be bothered wearing a coat. I was standing in line with a couple of friends and a few thousand other people. We were waiting to enter the newly remodeled dance club S4 on its opening night just before Christmas.

Once we entered, I felt like I was in Babylon, the club on *Queer as Folk*. The small entry opened into a two-story dance floor with intricate lights spinning above. Catwalks and balconies hung above as eager patrons watched the crush below. In back was a smaller, darker room where barely dressed men danced in cages.

The club contained more innocuous rooms, too, with pool tables and an outdoor patio. Upstairs, a glassed-in space held comfortable leather couches. My group planted ourselves there. I was exhilarated, having never experienced anything quite like this before.

And, then, suddenly, there was Sean Baugh, the guy who was kicked out of OBU back in 1993. I hadn't seen him since. We spotted each other at the same time, but he was the first to speak.

"Scott Jones!" he yelled. "Imagine running into you here. I guess I always knew you were gay, too."

I grabbed him in a big hug and responded, "I do remember one time when I was in your dorm room and was looking at your *International Male* catalog. You said something then about only gay men lingered over it."

He laughed. "That was a long time ago."

We grabbed vodka cranberries and sat down to catch up. He heard all about my life and shared with me about his. How he had transferred to another school and had to retake a number of classes. He had only been a semester away from graduating when OBU kicked him out. After college, he had moved to Dallas.

I had this rush, like everything in my life was coming together. That night at S4 was just a few days shy of the anniversary of that evening with John when I took my own first big step into the open. The year had been incredibly difficult and painful, but right now some things seemed to be going better. And here was Sean, the person who in so many ways had started it all.

I told him that. "You know, it was that experience of OBU kicking you out that really affected me," I said. "I became a public opponent of the school's policy."

He smiled and shook his head. "It's funny, because I don't really think about it anymore. I think it was more of a turning point for you and Matt Cox than it was for me."

"In so many ways, that was the first chapter in my coming out story. And now, running into you tonight, it's like everything is coming full circle."

But Sean didn't seem interested in a sentimental walk with me down memory lane; he was out to drink and dance and have fun. He introduced me to his friend Kendell, with whom I soon got into a long conversation. He was fascinated by theology, and we discussed my favorite theologians James McClendon, Stanley Hauerwas, and John Howard Yoder.

When alcohol service stopped at two a.m., everyone spilled onto the dance floor. Kendell and I were pushed together in this surging mass of male bodies as the lights flashed overhead. Eventually, we left together and made our way to my car. I took him home with me.

As I lay there, Kendell's sleeping, naked body wrapped around mine, I felt the excitement of having done something I'd never done before. And enjoyed it. The next morning, I drove Kendell back to his car and then returned home to get ready for church. It was Christmas Eve, after all.

"John may be having second thoughts."

It was New Year's Eve and I was on the phone with Sarah. I had to ask her to repeat herself.

"You heard me. He mentioned it at Christmas," she said.

"I don't know what to do with that," I responded. "I'm done and moving on, and suddenly he reappears?"

"I know," she answered. "But I think he really is serious."

I had spent months in therapy and suddenly this new information melted all the resolve I'd built up to move on. I was thrown into a strange mix of confusion, doubt, and hope. I wasn't ready to accept the possibility that John and I could reconcile.

A few weeks later I came home from seeing *Hotel Rwanda* by myself to a message on my answering machine from my

friend Tim telling me to read John's blog. Doubtful, I called
Tim and asked what was up.

"John has written you a letter of apology on his blog," Tim
told me.

I considered the various implications of that fact. *Did John
want to get back together? Did I? Why did he write publicly? Why
didn't he contact me directly?*

Tim told me I needed to read the letter. I responded that
I hadn't read his blog since May and wasn't sure I wanted to.
I added, "I've really worked hard at moving on."

Tim agreed, but reminded me that I had sent John a letter of
apology and this appeared to be John's response.

I sighed. "Yeah, but I sent it to *him*; I didn't post a letter of
apology on my blog." I asked why he hadn't just sent it to me
personally.

Of course Tim didn't know the answer to that puzzle, but he
gently reminded me, "He is apologizing, no matter what form
it has taken. Focus on that." Then Tim suggested that maybe
John wanted all our mutual friends to see the apology.

Suddenly alarmed at the possibility of being outed, I asked,
"Does he mention me by name?"

"No, but it's obvious to everyone who knows both of you that
he's talking about you." Then in his most encouraging tone,
Tim said, "Read it. Hang up, right now, and read it."

Before I could respond, he added, "But don't make any stupid
decisions. You need to read the apology, but that doesn't mean
you need to open yourself to more heartache."

I'd already sat down in front of my computer and opened
the internet. I clicked the link to John's blog, and there in front

of me was this post, full of explanation and apology. Reading those contrite words was good.

I called him. His voicemail picked up, so I left a message saying that I had read the apology. I thanked him for it.

He called forty-five minutes later.

"Hi," I said.

"Hi." It was his first spoken word to me since the previous May. "I got your message," he said.

"I read your blog post. Thank you," I responded.

"You're welcome." Then, after a breath he continued, "You deserved an apology. I'm so sorry. I was mean. I jerked you around and left you hanging. Last year I was confused and afraid and anxious and I lashed out. I should have never treated you that way."

Amazed and suddenly hopeful, I tried to apologize as well. "I'm sorry for everything I did—"

But he interrupted me. "It was good to get your letter of apology a few weeks ago. That's what got me thinking again."

"You're welcome," I said. "And I'm serious about what I wrote. It took therapy to realize, but I laid too many expectations on you. I created this whole fantasy and fell for it, and there was no way anyone could have lived up to all that." Then I softly added, "I'm sorry."

Our confessions were followed by catching up. We talked for two hours. Near the end of the call, we committed to calling regularly and renewing our friendship. John left open the possibility of more, but he cautioned that we'd need to take it easy and see what happens.

And then he said, "I love you."

I couldn't answer. My heart raced. My thoughts were a jumble. *Was he really saying these magic words now after everything that had transpired between us?* And, yet, hearing those words was good.

Did I love him? I wasn't sure, but only one response was possible. "I love you, too," I said.

15

"Aren't you ready to be fully out?"

I was driving south along I-35 on my way to Austin for a youth summer camp planning meeting with Scot Pankey, the youth minister at Cathedral of Hope in Dallas and an out gay man. We were discussing my job and the tenuous situation I'd found myself in.

Like me, Scot had grown up a Southern Baptist. We had met when he visited Royal Lane soon after I moved to Dallas and before he took the youth minister job at Cathedral of Hope.

Cathedral of Hope billed itself as the world's largest Christian church with a primary outreach to lesbian, gay, bisexual, and transgender persons. In the 1990s, under the leadership of the Rev. Michael Piazza, the congregation grew to over three thousand. This rapid growth occurred during the years of the AIDS crisis, when the church was performing as many as eight funerals a week. Mike said later that the congregation lost a thousand members to AIDS during those years.

The irony that the world's largest gay church was in conservative Dallas, Texas was lost on no one.

I was still in grad school when I first heard of Cathedral of Hope on my morning commute from Shawnee to Norman.

The architect Phillip Johnson was interviewed on NPR,
describing his vision for the cathedral he was designing for
them. Johnson wanted a building unlike anything else in
existence. White, undulating walls would organically rise from
the ground. Natural light would enter near the ceiling and flow
down the curvaceous sides. He desired to build a stunning
visual and spiritual symbol of a new and renewed faith.

Johnson's description of the planned building was breathtak-
ing, but I was really wowed when I learned about the gay-in-
clusive nature of the church. I decided right then, driving along
the back roads of central Oklahoma, that when the cathedral
was built, I would make a pilgrimage to see it. In 2005, while
I was living in Dallas, Johnson's cathedral had yet to be built.

That year Scot was determined to find a summer camp for the
CoH youth to attend. He was aware of the Alliance of Baptists,
the more liberal of the two groups that split away from the
Southern Baptist Convention after the fundamentalist takeover.
Unlike the more moderate Cooperative Baptist Fellowship, the
Alliance had decided to welcome and affirm gays and lesbians.

Scot's search connected him with a church in Austin and
eventually our camping group. He was invited to attend our
winter planning meeting, at which we would decide whether
to offer a formal invitation to the Cathedral of Hope. When
Scot learned that Royal Lane was part of the group and that
I would be attending the planning meeting, he called me and
we decided to ride down together.

Suddenly our network of Baptist churches was abuzz with the
news that CoH wanted to join us for camp, and not all of the
buzz was supportive. Though many of the churches in the group

were more progressive, few of them were officially open and affirming of LGBT persons. Inviting the non-Baptist, politically activist, and predominately LGBT Cathedral of Hope would be a big step. Many of us young progressives viewed the decision as a potential sea change moment for Baptists. We were ready to make our vote for LGBT inclusion.

On the drive, we talked about my situation at Royal Lane. "I thought last summer's agreement with Ray would buy me time in which I could find another job or make some plans," I said. "But I haven't done anything. I've been too focused on my personal issues—going to therapy, getting well from my depression, and dealing with coming out to family and friends."

"But aren't you afraid that something will happen, that you'll get outed and lose your job?" he asked.

Of course I was afraid of precisely this outcome. I told Scot about my fears.

"So what are you doing about it?" he asked.

"Well, nothing at this point," I admitted. The direct question had put me on the spot. "I've been praying that God will give me a sign about what to do next. And because my brain doesn't seem to be working very well at the moment, I keep asking God to give me a big, flashing sign that makes the path obvious." Scot didn't laugh as I had expected, but sat quietly for a moment, as if he was thinking over my situation.

When Scot spoke again, that big, flashing sign appeared. "I just thought of something," he said. "Yesterday I learned that the pastor of our congregation in Oklahoma City is leaving and that they are looking. You would be perfect for that congregation."

And I immediately answered, "Yes, I would."

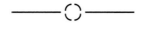

The Rev. Dr. Jo Hudson reached out to shake my hand as I entered her office at Cathedral of Hope. A confident woman in her fifties, Jo was soon to be installed as the new senior minister. Mike Piazza was still on staff, but they were in a transitional period.

In the middle of our car ride to Austin, Scot had called Jo and told her about me, declaring that I'd be a good person to pastor the Oklahoma City congregation. Jo arranged a meeting to get to know more about me and tell me about the job.

"I want to get to know you," Jo said as I followed her across her office. We took our seats beside a window, looking out at the trees. "But before you share your story, let me tell you a little bit about the job," she said. "No reason to waste our time, if you aren't interested or if it's not a good fit."

"Okay," I said, and smiled eagerly as I awaited her description.

"What we are looking for is someone with four qualities. First, he or she must be willing to move to Oklahoma and live there. Second, that someone must able to speak to Oklahomans in their cultural context. Third, he or she needs to be liberal in theology, but—and this is the fourth thing,—with an evangelical appreciation for worship. Do you think you fit those qualities?"

As I told many friends later, what jumped into my head was *You've maybe described only about five people in the entire country, and I'm one of them.* But that's not what I said.

Instead I controlled my excitement, looked her directly in the eye, and smiled my crooked smile.

"Yes, I do fit those qualities," I said. "Let me tell you about myself."

That meeting with Jo was soon followed by a more formal interview that also included Mike Piazza and the rest of the church's executive staff. They asked lots of questions about my sexual orientation, my coming out process, my theological and political views, and even who I had voted for in the presidential election of 2000. One of the staff members had researched me, and that research had included reading my blog.

The questions were unlike any I had experienced before in a job interview, especially the pointed, political ones. This was slightly off-putting and left me unsure as to whether I wanted to pursue the opportunity.

Also, if I pursued this position, I would be taking big steps—away from the denomination in which I had grown up and been nurtured, and out of the closet into the bright lights of being an activist for LGBT rights. Was I ready?

Mike Piazza had a commanding personality that made up for his small stature. When he spoke, he made the church's position very clear.

"We are looking for someone who is willing to be a public spokesperson for the LGBT community," he emphasized. "You would be fully out to everyone in your life. You would have to be willing to do media interviews and be engaged in public activism. You would have to accept being a target of animosity, hate, and maybe even the occasional threat of violence."

At the time I held leadership positions in the Cooperative Baptist Fellowship that promised more prominent, future roles in the denomination. But to hold onto that future, I'd have to remain in the closet. There weren't more than a handful of very liberal Baptist churches that might employ an openly gay pastor. Plus, I wasn't sure that I wanted to stay and struggle for full equality among Baptists.

A few months before, I had been in San Antonio attending the annual convention of the Baptist General Convention of Texas. Despite many of the fundamentalist leaders having come from Texas, the fundamentalists had never succeeded in taking control of the Texas state convention. The core theological principle of Texas Baptists, whether on the far left, the far right, or anywhere in between, seems to be "Don't tell me what to do."

The theme of that year's convention was "The Family of God" with an emphasis on diversity, particularly inclusion of Hispanics. But 2004 was the year of the Massachusetts Supreme Court ruling on same-sex marriage, and states across the country were voting on constitutional amendments to define marriage exclusively as being between one man and one woman. A resolution supporting that definition came before the Texas Baptist General Convention.

Around three thousand people sat in folding chairs that filled the cavernous hall of the San Antonio Convention Center. I sat with friends from Royal Lane. As the agenda was advancing toward the marriage resolution, Ray excused himself to go to the bathroom. I wondered if he was leaving to avoid the vote.

The chair called for debate on the marriage resolution. The children's minister from Highland Park Baptist Church in Austin spoke against the resolution, pointing out the irony of bringing such a divisive motion forward during a convention focused on the theme of celebrating the diverse family of

God. She said that no one doubted how most Texas Baptists felt on this issue, but that taking such a vote would only be a painful and cruel reminder to gays and lesbians that they were unwelcome.

The chair soon called the vote and instructed the convention to stand.

"All those voting in support?"

A loud rumble filled the room as thousands of chairs shifted. Almost every person in the cavernous hall rose to his or her feet.

"All those voting nay?" Ten people rose.

I sat back down and began to cry. I decided to walk out. A friend grabbed my arm and said "Don't let them see you cry. Don't be defeated."

But I couldn't help it. Tears rolling down my cheeks, I walked out.

I guess my interview at the Cathedral went well, because Mike Piazza called to say they wanted to set up a meeting with me and some of the members of the Oklahoma City congregation. He asked how soon I'd be able to go to Oklahoma City. I told him I'd already planned to go that weekend to celebrate my birthday. He arranged an interview for that Thursday night.

So on Thursday night, I met a dozen members of the Cathedral of Hope Oklahoma City. The host served homemade peppermint ice cream before we sat down in his living room to talk. They asked me questions, and I learned all about the church and their dreams. They wanted to proclaim an inclusive and welcoming Christianity, hoping to draw those disheartened by the exclusion experienced in many traditional churches. They wanted to provide hope and comfort to people suffering from discrimination at the hands of church, family, and society. They wanted people to know that it was okay to be gay.

I was impressed by their energetic and enthusiastic vision and their commitment to that vision. I left the interview feeling that it would be an honor to be their pastor. Plus, I enjoyed the homemade peppermint ice cream.

Cathedral of Hope OKC was founded in 2000, five years before my interview. Mike Piazza had noticed a significant number of Oklahomans visited Cathedral of Hope in Dallas. He concluded that there was an unmet need for an open and affirming church in Oklahoma City. He first organized a big Easter service to be held in Oklahoma City. They rented a bus and transported the choir and orchestra of the Dallas congregation to the special service. Three hundred people attended. A small home group formed soon after, and in 2000, the Oklahoma City congregation began weekly worship with its own pastor, the Rev. Kevin McLemore. Those Sunday-night services were held in the First Unitarian Church's sanctuary.

Rev. McLemore only stayed two years, and by 2005 the growing congregation had been served by two full-time pastors and one year-long interim. To create stability, they needed a pastor who was willing to stay. Current membership at that time was around one hundred, and average weekly attendance was about half that.

During the interview, one of the church members asked me how the church could grow.

I was ready with an answer. "If we are faithful—in our worship and education, our giving and our service, in our caring and our fellowship, in all the ways we are church—then God will use us to fulfill God's mission," I said. "I think you have a chance to be powerful witnesses for the gospel in a very conservative Oklahoma, and to really help change things."

The people around the room smiled widely.

Pastoring Cathedral of Hope OKC would be very different from what I was used to. I had grown up in larger churches and served in multi-staff settings. We had eleven people on staff at Royal Lane. At Cathedral of Hope OKC, I'd be the only full-time person with help from a part-time director of music. Everything else was done by volunteers or by staff at Cathedral of Hope Dallas, which still coordinated most tasks for the fledgling Oklahoma City congregation. The weekly worship bulletins were laid out, printed, and shipped to Oklahoma City by staff members in Dallas. Their accountants did all the bookkeeping and kept the financial records. All advertising and publicity came from Dallas.

So on the one hand, I'd be pastoring a small congregation that was determined to grow, but I would technically be on staff with almost thirty other people at this very large church, so I'd be able to draw upon their resources, abilities, and technologies. At least that was how the job was presented to me during those initial conversations.

Did the opportunity actually exist for me to be at home in Oklahoma, live as an out gay man, and work as a minister? I'd never thought these three things could be true at the same time.

Thrilled by that possibility, I prepared for my birthday

dinner on Friday night. The dinner was at Pearl's Lakeside, a Cajun-style seafood place that overlooked Lake Hefner in northwest Oklahoma City. As I walked up to the restaurant's entrance, I spotted John outside smoking a cigarette with his sister Sarah. I felt excited and nervous to see him for the first time since our breakup.

He said, "Hi."

I smiled and said, "Hi."

He finished his cigarette and we all walked into the restaurant together.

During dinner, we watched the setting sun as light glistened on the water. Nineteen people attended. Chris, with his roguish smile. My uncle Frank. Harley came with Debra, who was looking great in a colorful blouse. A few old friends from college where there, along with some of my new blog friends. Mom was jubilant, sharing the news with everyone about how my interview had gone. Even my sister Erin and her husband Adam came. I moved about the tables, chatting with everyone.

John and I went for coffee together after dinner. I was anxious, but it felt good to finally be sitting across from him alone, even if we were surrounded by the bright lighting, garish colors, and noisy patrons of an IHOP at night.

John said, "Meeting your sister was strange."

"Yeah," I responded. "For me, introducing you two was the strangest moment of the evening."

"It took all my self-control not to claw her eyes out," he said, grinning and arching his eyebrows.

I laughed. "I can understand. You did very well. Both of you. Very surface polite."

John refilled our mugs with coffee as I continued. "The whole evening was so exciting for me," I said. "All those family members and new friends, and here were you and Erin, both in the same place together. A year ago I would never have imagined all of those people being in the same place."

He took a sip of his coffee. "I know. You never thought your mother would be okay with you being gay. You worried that by this point you'd have no family left and probably no job, either. I remember your anxieties."

"But all of that's gone tonight. I feel triumphant. Maybe tonight's a sign from God?" I was pretty excited.

"I don't know if I'd go that far, but I know what you mean. I understand why it feels that way." He grinned again, that grin I delighted in. My anxieties about the possibility of our reconciliation were beginning to melt away.

"After all the hard work and dark times of the past year, suddenly my life appears to be heading in the right direction." I meant more than the job. I waited for him to open a possibility.

But all he said was, "It is headed in the right direction. I'm happy for you."

On Monday, Mike Piazza called to say they'd decided not to finish the interviews with the other finalist—if I wanted the job. I would preach before the Oklahoma City congregation in April as the pastoral candidate, and the congregation would vote. We set up a meeting for me to come into the Dallas offices and finalize the arrangements.

That night, I wrote in my journal.

It seems that I am on the verge of everything in my life coming together!

16

The Dawn of a New Day

I was wearing the black academic robe given to me by some members of Royal Lane, with the blue trim indicating my PhD in philosophy. I was standing in this high, white pulpit, looking out over a room filled with smiling faces, most of whom I'd only just met the day before. The evening sun was shining through the tall, clear glass windows, filling the Colonial-style sanctuary with light.

My leather portfolio was open in front of me. Tucked inside its one pocket was a note a ministry colleague in Dallas had given to me just that week. The note read *Scott, you rock.* I looked down at it and touched it before beginning my sermon.

The Sunday after Easter, the lectionary provides the story of Doubting Thomas. So I preached on resurrection and doubts, sharing my own story of rising up from the depression of the year before.

"I think we have something special to say," I said as I built toward the conclusion of my sermon. "We who are gay and lesbian have gone through an experience that our heterosexual sisters and brothers haven't gone through. We have an extra rite of passage, an extra step in life's journey. You see, we have experienced our Good Fridays. Some of us have lain in the tomb for decades. But at some point, we grabbed hold of a new life. We have claimed a new hope.

"And what a journey it has been. Despite anxiety. Despite fear. Despite a path that seemed fraught with danger on every side. Despite a world full of many who would rob us of our dignity and break us. We came out. Despite all that, don't you also remember the excitement, the joy, the new sense of self-awareness, the new confidence? The timid early steps give way to pride. And suddenly we find ourselves at the dawn of a new day, entering new life.

"You who are family and friends, you too had your days of doubt. You too were filled with anxiety, fear, and grief. You had to make sense of this new thing. But you grasped that it was new life. You witnessed these journeys and blessed them and celebrated them. So I say to you that this is your story, too.

"These stories, our stories, are stories of resurrection."

After worship, the congregation served fried chicken in the dining hall and my twenty-one guests—family, friends, ministry colleagues, and John—milled about with the eager members of Cathedral of Hope Oklahoma City. The only small blemish on the night was that my sister had declined the invitation to join us.

John had cooked dinner for me at his new apartment two nights before. Because so much of his stuff had previously been in storage, I finally got to see many of his belongings. I scanned his book collection as he finished preparing dinner. The shelves were filled with Augusten Burroughs and David Sedaris, Anais Nin and J. K. Rowling. He had set the table using old 45 records as chargers.

I gave him a birthday present. *Their Eyes Were Watching God* was his favorite novel. I had found a Zora Neale Hurston scrapbook, filled with facsimiles of her notes and manuscripts, photos, a recording of her reading, and more. As he unwrapped the gift, his eyes sparkled with delight.

After dinner, we watched a *Harry Potter* film. When I was about to leave, I thanked him for having me over. He stood at the door, smiling through his goatee, looking cute. He wished me good luck with the sermon and the vote.

"Thanks," I said. "I can't believe how everything is changing and working out." I knew not to try to hug him, and he didn't hug me.

"See you Sunday," I said, and walked down the stairs and out to my car.

Once all the goodbyes had been said at church that night, I went looking for John. Sarah said he was walking home to his new apartment. The redbuds were in full bloom on a beautiful spring evening. I drove over to his apartment and sat in my car outside waiting for him to arrive. I was looking forward to talking over the day's experiences with him.

When John walked up and saw me sitting there, a look of alarm crossed his face. "What are you doing?" he asked.

Taken aback, I answered, "Well, I couldn't eat during the reception, because I was too busy talking to people. So I wondered if you might want to go to dinner with me and talk about the whole experience."

He hesitantly came closer and responded with more pointed questions. "You just drove over here and waited for me? How did you know I was walking home?"

Now worried that this situation was heading in a direction I could never have imagined, I gently explained, "Your sister told me that you were headed this way."

"I wish you'd called," he said, with a tone of disappointment. But after a reflective pause, he added, with some annoyance, "I guess you couldn't, since you still don't own a cell phone."

"Well, do you want to go to dinner?" I didn't understand why he was unsettled.

He looked around and then answered. "I am hungry. I guess so."

"Where do you want to go, then?" I was hoping that the awkward moment had passed.

"There's a Thai place nearby, how about there?" So he got in my car and we went to dinner. There was no further awkwardness. We chatted about the excitement of the church service and my impending move.

That week I was formally offered the job in Oklahoma City, and I accepted. John also quit answering calls or responding to emails. Again.

He finally called eight days later. "I can't do it, Scott," he said. "Why did you come sit outside my apartment in your car?"

"Because I was happy and wanted to share my joy with you," I said, hopeful that he would understand.

But he responded by saying, "You're so controlling."

I was taken aback. "How am I controlling? How is wanting to share my joy with you controlling? I don't even begin to understand that."

"You won't give me the space I need," he said in measured

tones. He didn't sound angry. He sounded disappointed. "You want things to move too quickly. I just can't do it."

None of what he said made any sense to me. Months of talking and e-mailing, the great time together having dinner at his apartment, his enthusiasm for me moving to Oklahoma City. And now he was stating unequivocally that he did not want to be with me. I was disappointed.

But I wasn't crushed. Too much was finally going well in my life. I wasn't going to retreat into the depression of the year before. I rubbed my forehead with my left hand as I pondered my response.

I sighed. "Fine," I said. "Then we're done. A relationship simply won't work between us."

John added, "Yes, we're finished." Was there some sadness in his voice? I believed there was.

There was a mix of sadness and resolution in my voice when I responded. "Okay then, John. Goodbye."

And he ended the conversation with "Goodbye, Scott" before hanging up.

I remained sitting quietly, my head in my hands, but I did not cry.

I had a new job. I was moving. And I was finally coming out fully and publicly.

Cathedral of Hope Dallas emailed their vast network to announce that I was the new pastor of the Oklahoma City congregation. We'd agreed upon a date for the announcement, but they sent the email two weeks before that date. I hadn't told everyone I had wanted to yet, and I hadn't announced my resignation to Royal Lane's congregation. I began receiving emails from Baptist clergy colleagues congratulating me on the new move, some asking to hear my story. I was amused and surprised to learn how many Baptist ministers were on Cathedral of Hope's email list.

When I read my letter of resignation to the Royal Lane congregation at the close of a worship service, I noticed more than one knowing nod of the head or glance at a spouse when I said which church I was going to serve.

Mary Lou, who had guided our hiking trip the summer before, came to my office a few days later. She hugged me and then sat down in the stuffed blue chair adjacent to my desk.

"I'm very happy for you," she said. "Congratulations."

Smiling, I replied, "Thank you. The last couple of years have been very interesting, and I'm excited about the next chapter in my life."

"I have a story to share with you," she said, grinning mischievously.

"Oh?" I asked, intrigued.

"When you first came to Royal Lane, I assumed you were gay. I went around telling all my friends how excited I was that our church had hired a gay minister." I laughed. "One day I was talking to another church member and sharing my excitement, and she said to me, 'Mary Lou, Scott's not out. I don't even know if he's figured it out himself yet.'"

I laughed some more.

"I was so embarrassed," she continued. "I had to go back to all those friends I'd told you were gay and tell them that you weren't out and that they weren't supposed to say anything about it. I'm glad that you are out now."

"Me too," I said. I enjoyed the story.

Then Mary Lou's grin faded. "While I'm very happy for you, I'm sad for our church that you are leaving." Before I could respond, she added, "And I'm also sad we don't get a chance to embrace your ministry with us as an openly gay man. I believe we were up to the challenge."

Mary Lou's story and comments were refreshing to hear. And they weren't exceptional. I learned in my remaining weeks at Royal Lane that many church members had children, siblings, or other family members who were gay. I learned that quite a few church members had figured out I was gay, or at least suspected it. I learned that many would have been fine with it.

But I also learned, indirectly, of a few others who wouldn't have been.

I believe God called me to Royal Lane. I'm convinced of the importance of my ministry there. One reason is the almost half-dozen teenagers from that youth group who have come out as LGBT in the decade since.

A month after I moved away, I received a text message from one of the fifteen year olds in the Royal Lane youth group asking if we could talk. I happened to be in Dallas at the time, so I told him I'd drop by to see him. He wanted to go for a drive, and as we did, he told me he was gay. Over the course of the next few months, whenever I was in town we'd spend time together. I got to introduce him to things that had only recently been introduced to me. I took him to a bookstore and showed him gay magazines like *The Advocate* and *Out* and the gay and lesbian section of books. I took him down to the gayborhood one afternoon, and we hung out at the coffee shop. I answered his many questions.

He was from a very supportive family, but wasn't quite ready to talk to them about his identity. Being his friend and mentor during this process, I realized how much the world was changing. He had reached adolescence, realized his sexuality, and then began to act on it. No years of passing and hiding in the closet, pretending to be something he wasn't. The experience of coming out as gay was in the midst of a dramatic transformation.

In 2010, Royal Lane Baptist Church officially became an open and affirming congregation, stating publicly that LGBT persons were welcome in the church. As a result, the Baptist General Convention of Texas kicked them out. A handful of church members departed the congregation, but even more new members came. Ray was now the Pastor Emeritus and supported the action. Harry was one of the strongest advocates for it and celebrated the decision.

In the months after I came out publicly and moved to Oklahoma City, I experienced discrimination from my moderate Baptist colleagues.

I intended to continue my work on the Local Arrangements Committee for the annual meeting of the Cooperative Baptist Fellowship, as we were only a couple of months away from the event. My friend Tim Youmans, who was part of the team of colleagues I had drawn together to help me with the youth portion of the national meeting, offered to step in if I needed him to. But I had put a lot of work into the program and didn't want to dump the event on someone else at the last moment.

About three weeks before the General Assembly was to convene, I received a phone call from two national officers of the Cooperative Baptist Fellowship, two people I had worked with on a handful of projects. They asked me if what they'd heard was true, that I had moved to Cathedral of Hope. When I told them I had, they asked me to resign. My new church's involvement in Gay Pride would be problematic for them, they explained. They couldn't have the chair of their Youth event involved in such things.

There was no reason to argue or fight. I told them I understood. I did understand, but that didn't make the moment any easier. I resigned and Tim took over the event.

So much for the Cooperative Baptist Fellowship. At the time of this writing, the group remains stuck due to its wishy-washy lack of conviction. On the issue of gay equality, the wider American culture is fast leaving the CBF behind and making it irrelevant.

At the winter planning meeting for that summer's youth camp, the Southwest Baptist Youth Camping Association had voted to invite the Cathedral of Hope in Dallas to participate in camp. After I announced my new job and came out in April, some members of some of the churches objected to welcoming a pre-dominantly LGBT church into the camping group. One church, Rolling Hills Baptist Church in Fayetteville, Arkansas, pulled out of the camping association because of the decision. Their decision was quite painful, as I had previously served as youth minister at Rolling Hills. I realized that their decision about camp was partly motivated by hurt and anger that some of those church members felt toward me over my own coming out.

I had remained close to a handful of families from Rolling Hills. When I came out, some of them cut me off. I've been told by other families who remained close to me that the reaction of those families was partly because they were hurt that I didn't tell them in person. I regret that I was unable to share my story with them personally, but in the few weeks between accepting the job in Oklahoma City and coming out, I didn't have time to make the five hour drive to Fayetteville and tell everyone I cared about in person. Instead, I wrote letters. I know it wasn't ideal. Over the course of three weeks, I went from being mostly in the closet to announcing publicly that I was a gay man. Those weeks were exhilarating and exhausting. And unfortunately, not everyone learned the truth in the best way.

A few of the senior ministers of the camping association churches—ministers who had not attended the winter planning meeting—criticized the decision of those of us who had been there and voted for inviting the Cathedral of Hope to attend. The Senior Pastor of First Baptist Austin wrote an angry email to the camping group charging that I had manipulated the entire thing. He said I had convinced my colleagues to vote for including Cathedral of Hope because I was in the process of moving there, and that I had kept my move a secret. In a reply to that email, a fellow youth minister informed that angry pastor that the vote to invite Cathedral of Hope to camp had been taken before I had even applied for the job. He added that I wasn't the person who had invited Cathedral of Hope to the planning meeting in the first place. In other words, he refuted the false information of the Austin pastor. I never received an apology from that minister, even though he had attacked my integrity and lied about me. I was disappointed and deeply hurt as many ministers I had respected and counted as friends distanced themselves from me and demonstrated a lack of integrity.

So in a few short weeks, I was cast off by the Baptists who had nurtured me my entire life.

17

Because We Can

A week after I left Royal Lane, I began blogging elements of my coming out story. Suddenly, my blog was receiving one thousand daily views. People were reading my story, asking questions, and offering words of support. At a coffee shop in Oklahoma City my first week back in town, I ran into a former college classmate who was a Southern Baptist minister.

"Welcome back," he said. "I've been reading your blog. Congratulations and good luck."

People started coming out to me. Among them were other ministers—some of whom were married to opposite-sex spouses—college classmates, and fellow Oklahoma Baptist University alums. I began to realize that a new ministry was opening for me; I was going to be able to help other people in their journeys out. Sharing my story was helping other people share theirs, and it was giving some of them inspiration to courageously begin coming out. It felt surreal that all these people were outing themselves to me, because I was only just then coming out of the closet myself.

Upon my return to Oklahoma I immediately became an advocate and activist for LGBT justice and equality. My first advocacy appearance was at an Oklahoma City Public Schools board meeting where some LGBT leaders were trying to amend the school's anti-bullying and anti-discrimination policies to include protections for LGBT students.

Joe Quigley was spearheading the initiative. With his scruffy beard and long, greying hair pulled back in a ponytail, the longtime English teacher looked like an old hippie. He had a booming voice, and he knew how to use it. He also drew wickedly funny caricatures of local politicians. Joe had begun this battle for an amended anti-bullying policy almost a decade before, after one of his students committed suicide as a result of being bullied.

At the meeting I was introduced to Paul Thompson, a veteran Oklahoma City gay activist who had defied anti-gay laws in the1960s. Back then, police would intimidate gay men by raiding bars and arresting the people inside. Most people would pay the fine and get out of jail, hoping to keep the arrest a secret. Paul was the first person in Oklahoma City to fight his arrest. That meant the story went public. He won his case—a big step in the gay rights struggle in Oklahoma.

Paul had participated in almost every LGBT organization in the region. He had also served for many decades on the local NAACP chapter's board of directors, even though he was white. His life's work had been to build the coalition necessary for achieving LGBT civil rights.

A year into knowing Paul, I began to recognize something about his attire. When I asked him about it, he explained his fashion choice to me. Years before he had acquired a wardrobe of the eight colors of the original rainbow flag—hot pink, red, orange, yellow, green, turquoise, indigo, and violet. Each day he wore one of those colors, cycling back to the beginning on the ninth day. Over the years friends had given him gifts, building his collection of shirts, belts, and socks for each of the eight colors.

Paula Sophia was the one who had invited me to join her at that Oklahoma City Public Schools board meeting. She was a church member and an Oklahoma City police officer who had transitioned from male to female a few years before. Her transition was a big local news story. Paula was also a military veteran and an ordained Episcopal deacon, a slam poet, and an author working on her first novel.

A few weeks before, she and I had gone to dinner in order to get better acquainted. I was living with my parents at the time while waiting for my house in Dallas to sell, and Mom and I were watching TV in the den as I waited for Paula to pick me up.

"You know," I said, "I've never really interacted with a transgender person before. I'm a little nervous that I'll say or do something wrong. I'm not sure how I'm supposed to act. I have lots of questions, but it seems rude to ask them."

Mom turned away from the news she was watching on television and looked at me. "I'm sure you'll do fine," she said. "Paula is a really nice lady." They had met a few times during my first weeks back in Oklahoma City.

When I returned from dinner later that night, Mom asked me how it had gone.

"Actually, the dinner was great," I said. "I wasn't nervous at all after a few minutes. You know why?"

I told her I had realized that I should simply treat Paula like I would any other person. "It's such an obvious thing," I said. "I felt really dumb for being nervous ahead of time."

Mom smiled her knowing smile, as if she had left me to figure out this simple truth on my own. She was surprising me by how open she was to my new life and all the new people and experiences my return to Oklahoma had brought into hers.

I, too, had much to learn.

The gay community possesses unique language, rules, and etiquette.

Early on, I was walking through a mall with a gay friend when a gay male couple walked past us.

"They're family," my friend said.

I responded, "No, they're a gay couple." The friend explained that "family" was a euphemism for "gay."

Another friend criticized me for not folding and holding my dollar bill appropriately when tipping a drag queen. He then taught me how to do it. You need to loosely fold the bill in half the long way and then, with your middle finger inside the fold and your two adjacent fingers outside the fold, hold onto one end and stick the bill forward.

Learning how to follow instead of lead when dancing was strange to me. But since I have never been the most coordinated person or a very good dancer, I must say I prefer following.

I was learning at church as well. For one thing, LGBT folk are more demonstrative. Oklahomans are pretty demonstrative to begin with, so gay Oklahomans really are. Handshakes at church were uncommon because hugs were the norm. And most people would also give you a peck on the cheek. Over the years this casual kissing became such a common experience for me that one time I gave a peck on the cheek to one of the straight men who attended church, and I quickly apologized.

"No problem," he said. "I got used to that at this church a long time ago."

I had never worn the fancy vestments that were the norm at the Cathedral of Hope. We wore a white alb and tied it with a cincture, which is basically a rope belt. Church member Frances Ann taught me how to tie the cincture properly. We also wore chasubles—the big flowing pieces that go over albs and look like something a bishop would wear. I quickly learned how gay all this dressing up felt. Clerical vestments really are a form of drag.

Besides the robes, their order of worship was new to me. Cathedral of Hope observed a more formal liturgy than the other congregations I had served. The liturgy included weekly communion as opposed to the monthly communion I had grown accustomed to. I had to learn their movements and the words. And I had to start singing regularly, as their tradition was to use sung communion liturgies during different seasons of the year. Other than when I'm showering, I've never been a soloist, so soloing in public was an intimidating idea. After my first feeble attempt, one kind congregant told me he liked the "natural quality" of my voice.

Cathedral of Hope had been a member of the Metropolitan Community Churches and maintained two lovely communion traditions from the MCC. First, couples or entire families would gather around the minister to receive communion instead of each person coming forward individually. Also, after receiving communion, the minister would give a lengthier blessing than is common in other traditions. The longer blessing could turn into praying with the family, particularly if one knew of a special need.

But most new to me was the way Cathedral of Hope served communion, with the minister dipping the wafer in the wine and then placing the wafer on the tongue of the congregant. Of course various denominations serve communion this way, but I never had. Which led to a surprise the first time I did so.

It was a Sunday morning at Cathedral of Hope Dallas when I was introduced as the new Oklahoma City minister. Almost one thousand people were in attendance in worship, which was the first time I had been in a room with so many LGBT people. Being in that huge crowd of people like me was thrilling. I should also confess that I was repeatedly distracted while leading worship because I kept noticing so many good-looking gay men in attendance.

When communion began, I was standing at the front of the sanctuary with the other ministers as the congregants moved up the aisles toward us. Suddenly, some of those very good-looking men I had been noticing were standing right in front of me, opening their mouths and sticking their tongues out. I had never experienced serving communion as erotic before.

Fortunately I got used to serving communion this way, and it was not a weekly distraction.

I did enjoy being in a religious setting that wasn't uptight about sex and eroticism. Church members joked and laughed about sexual innuendo and didn't expect their minister to be a prude. My music director, Bob, even took me shopping at one of the erotica stores in Oklahoma City to make sure I was well-stocked with the appropriate lubes, condoms, etc. After a lifetime as a Baptist, I was experiencing liberation.

I immersed myself in queer theology and biblical scholarship. Writing my sermon every week became a fun, creative experience in seeing the possibilities of applying ancient stories to my congregation and their lives as LGBT persons in very conservative, evangelical Oklahoma. The best example was the sermon I preached on Pride Weekend that year, in which I explored the spiritual meanings of gay camp.

"But what is the significance of our lighter moments, our silliness, our camp? Why do we enjoy laughing at *The L Word*, *Queer as Folk*, and *Will and Grace*? Why do we dress up and engage in rituals like the rodeo, drag shows, and clubbing? Why do we fill our conversations with tacky humour and play to stereotypes?

"Largely, because we can. It is our expression of freedom. Because we are an oppressed people, our lives are filled with absurdity. So in response, we have played up the absurd and enjoyed every minute of it. The world forces closeted gays to perform and wear masks, and so we do it for fun and enjoyment."

I participated in my first gay pride festival and parade. The festival was held in Memorial Park along Classen Boulevard in Oklahoma City. Rainbow flags were flying and the park was filled with happy people—couples holding hands, parents pushing strollers, packs of teenagers. Gay cowboys and lesbians in leather, young gay boys in short shorts and tight t-shirts, and middle-aged drag queens in big hair and jewelry mingled together while elderly women sat on folding chairs under the shade trees watching it all. Our church's booth was near the swings, and I enjoyed the childish delight of swinging.

On Sunday afternoon, the parade assembled on Classen Boulevard in front of the park. Our congregation was handing out bottles of water along the parade route. The sun blazed from a cloudless sky. Plunging my hands into the ice chests and bringing up the dripping bottles refreshed me from the heat. As the parade advanced, I was running back and forth from the truck to the curb grabbing more bottles from the ice chests and handing them out to the grateful spectators who lined the street.

As we came down 39th Street, the numbers of people watching from the front yards of houses increased. Then the parade crested a hill and descended toward the intersection of 39th and Penn, heading toward the gay strip. From that crest, I could see the tens of thousands of people who had swarmed the area. Suddenly, as we moved forward, I was engulfed in a mass of cheering, queer humanity. It felt like they were cheering for me. I hopped up to stand in the back of the truck, and as we entered that throng, I spread my arms wide, smiled broadly, and soaked up the energy and the joy.

18

"*I am not a social ill.*"

"So, what do you think we should do for dinner?" I asked.

He looked up from his desk. I was sitting on a couch on the other side of his office. I had taken my glasses off and was polishing them on the tail of my shirt, not realizing at the time that a little of my belly hair was exposed. He told me later that he had noticed the hair and was turned on.

He was the finance director at the Cathedral of Hope in Dallas. This was my first extended visit to the church offices, a time for me to get to know the staff and learn about their work. I was technically a staff member there, even though I was pastoring the Oklahoma City parish. This dual role required me to spend time every week in Dallas. So for those first few months, I felt as if I hadn't moved. I slept in my own bed at my Dallas house, which was still on the market, and hung out with my old friends from Royal Lane. Most weeks I still had dinner on Wednesdays with the same group of people I'd met with each week when I lived there.

As Dean of Cathedral of Hope and my boss, Mike Piazza told me to go around to each office at the church and meet the staff to discuss their work and learn how they could help me in mine. I met the ministry coordinator, who gave me forms to fill out and return to her each time we held an event so she could track the participants and results. I met the communications director, who reminded me that any public relations materials needed to go through his staff. I met another new staffer, a young man working on financial development who discussed the need for my congregation to raise more money to cover its expenses. The minister who oversaw benevolence and service projects didn't think he'd be of much help to me, what with me pastoring hundreds of miles away. I met the music director, who told me about the church's commitment to gender-inclusive hymns, and the graphic designer who designed our weekly bulletins who gave me instructions on the production timeline. Then, finally, I met the finance director. He explained how to request reimbursements and told me about the church's budget and bookkeeping system. It was in his office where I found myself lingering.

The room was filled with houseplants and symbols of various religions, including a Ganesh statue on the sideboard. Against the back wall, under a plate-glass window with a view of trees and a dirty creek, was a sleeping couch with pillows, bolsters, and a throw.

He was in his late thirties, with light blond hair and a moustache. Not long into our conversation about church finances, I noticed that he was grinning playfully. Our conversation soon shifted to a larger discussion of the church and our ministry. He wanted to hear more about me and my sense of calling. My story prompted him to share elements of his, including his passion for Cathedral of Hope.

I'd spent no more than ten or fifteen minutes in the other offices. But after two hours had passed I was still sitting on his couch, enjoying a conversation that was becoming increasingly flirtatious. I could tell he was enjoying it, too, so I decided we should make dinner plans.

His grin grew even bigger and his eyes sparkled. He told me he had plans with friends and invited me to join them.

We went to a Mexican restaurant not far from the church. John's friends, Jason and Paul, were fun guys who shared a few knowing glances that indicated they'd caught onto what was clearly developing into a date. After dinner, they quickly departed. As we approached my car and I was wondering if the evening was about to end, he spun me around and kissed me, his moustache tickling my upper lip.

After the kiss, as he pulled away, I looked into his blue eyes and said, "John, do you want to see my house?"

Of course this cute, flirtatious guy shared a name with my ex.

John drove a red truck and lived in a condo not far from the church and the gayborhood. He had co-owned a floral business with his ex before their business, and then their relationship, collapsed during the post-9/11 economic downturn.

The first time I came to stay with him, he surprised me with a bouquet of flowers that he had arranged himself. This was the first time any romantic interest had ever given me flowers.

John then showed me around his condo. The bedroom was dominated by a California king-sized bed. I sat my bag down, and as I turned toward him, he grabbed me and kissed me hard. Then he pushed me onto his big bed, climbed on top of me, and began unbuttoning my shirt.

He later treated me to a nice dinner.

John's condo became something of a retreat in those early months of transition from Dallas to Oklahoma City, while I was living with my parents. The space was quiet and comfortable, filled with plants and rich fabrics.

Teasing each other in bed a few weeks into the relationship, I slipped and called him by my ex's last name, not his. My immediate apologies didn't comfort him. Nor did Paul and Jason's repeated assurances that it was really a reasonable mistake. Second John never quite forgave me that one.

Understandable, really. He was justified in thinking that I was still enamored of my ex. The first time I spent the night at his condo, after the flowers and the nice dinner, I'd cried about how damaged I still felt over that break-up with First John. I was frightened of falling too fast and getting hurt. So cliché, really, but I was overwhelmed by those emotions.

He just held me and reassured me. "I'm not that John."

Because I was so sensitive, he took to calling me his "Fragile Flower." Because of my clumsy tendency to trip and fall, he also called me "Grace."

John visited Oklahoma City now and then for a weekend, and we always arranged for him to stay in some church member's guest room. We didn't want to push Mom's goodwill too far.

The night of the Oklahoma City Pride Parade, we went out to the gay strip to drink. I had this fantasy that my first Pride festival would be like Justin's on *Queer as Folk*—in the midst of all the festivities, he and Brian meet in the middle of the street and kiss as the camera spins around them and away.

My experience wasn't anything like that. We were exhausted

from the long day—festival, parade, then church service—and hadn't been out long before John wanted to leave. He said he was tired. I was disappointed and became grumpy on the drive back to the guest room we were using that weekend. John became frustrated with my grumpiness and finally asked what was wrong.

I told him about my fantasy.

"I'm sorry," he said. "But life isn't quite like that."

"I know," I said, acknowledging reality, but still disappointed. Then he held me close and said, "I love you."

His words surprised me. I still wasn't sure how I felt about him. But I'd once said the big words, and they weren't reciprocated. I knew that felt like shit. I didn't want to hurt him.

So I said, "I love you too."

That summer, the Metro Library Commission responded to a complaint from a freshman state legislator named Sally Kern about gay-themed books in the children's section of the public library. The offending book was *King and King*, a children's picture book about a young prince who falls in love not with a princess, but rather with another prince. The book had won awards, but also the ire of religious conservatives across the country.

Kern was new on the public scene. A short, dowdy woman who rarely smiled, she had been a high school government teacher before running for the state legislature. Her district was originally settled by Nazarenes, a Holiness branch of Christianity, which resulted in it being the most conservative pocket of Oklahoma City. Kern herself was a Southern Baptist.

Her husband pastored a church near downtown that was known for helping the poor.

Kern wanted *King and King* and all books like it banned. She had filed her complaint after one of her constituents, a mother, discovered *King and King* among a handful of books her child had brought home from the library.

The library commission held a series of meetings that year to consider her complaint. I arrived in Oklahoma City in the midst of this controversy and began attending the monthly meetings as the issue was debated. I was interviewed by a local news reporter at the first one I attended.

Being a spokesperson in the press was not something I had previously identified as a necessary skill for Christian ministry, but that summer I received a crash course. I was on television twice, I was featured on the cover of the local LGBT newspaper, and I was interviewed in an hour-long radio show about religion and LGBT issues. Mike Piazza had been right that I'd be thrust into the public eye and that I'd have to be a spokesperson for both the church and the greater LGBT community.

Oklahoma City's LGBT community was fortunate to have an out public official serving on the library commission. Jim Roth was an Oklahoma County Commissioner who had been an out gay man when he was elected to office. Jim was young, smart, and good looking, with one of those wide, bright smiles that helps in political life. He was proving to be a competent and highly respected public official. Of course he was opposed to any attempt to ban books, and his presence helped to guarantee that outcome was never seriously considered.

At the public hearing on this issue, I experienced for the first time the vitriol that anti-gay forces can unleash. Kern and her supporters, who included some Christian ministers, denounced homosexuality as sinful and made vile claims including child abuse, rampant spread of disease, and social corruption. Most surprising was that they would look for books with sexual content in the library's adult section and read excerpts from these into the public record. I found their hypocrisy stunning. If you really thought such things contributed to the corruption of society, why would you read them out loud at a public gathering in front of television cameras?

Few of the commissioners favored banning the books outright, and some opposed any change to the library's practices. Some of those in the middle seemed to hold anti-gay positions. I suspected that these commissioners wanted to support the ban, but were made uncomfortable by the public attention. "The courage of their bigotry" is a phrase I coined to describe those who spoke their anti-gay opinion out loud so we could directly contest it.

The debates revealed how ignorant some of the library commissioners were of libraries and their practices. For instance, one commissioner asked the director of libraries why these sorts of books weren't simply placed on a high shelf, out of reach of children. She looked confused and answered, "There aren't any high shelves in the children's sections of the libraries. The point is for the books to be accessible to children."

The final outcome was described as a compromise. To make access more difficult, the books would be placed in a special section in each library's children's section. One of the commissioners wanted it noted that he preferred they select a top shelf. Instead of directing attention only to books that might have gay themes, books addressing all sorts of topics would be included, such as divorce, addiction, sexual abuse, and family violence. Basically any topic that the conservative commissioners thought was controversial.

The compromise pleased no one, including Kern and her cohorts who wanted a ban. The progressives were angered at these exceptions from standard library practices. I noticed that most of the library staff in the meeting seemed resigned to an outcome that was better than it might have been. I saw a few of them sigh.

My anger came out in the final meeting when the proposal to establish this compromise was voted on. Testifying before the commission, I said, "I am not an abuser of children. I am not a sexual abuser. I am not guilty of domestic or family violence. I am not an abuser of drugs or medication. I am not a social ill. Nor should I be equated with such."

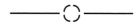

Hanging out at John's condo in Dallas, we would often curl up on his couch together to watch the final episodes of *Queer as Folk* as they aired that summer. In one, the nightclub Babylon is bombed. John held me close as we finished watching that episode, and our mood was sober.

"You know," John said, "We have high security at the church because of this very fear."

"I know about the high security," I said. "They have educated me about it."

The main offices of the church were located at the rear

of the building. They could only be accessed with an electronically coded card. The receptionist's desk was located in an area outside the front doors of the actual building and attached via a breezeway. During the work week, any visitors to the building were escorted from the reception area to the main offices.

Uniformed security guards patrolled the grounds during worship services and big events. The ushers were also trained in how to respond to a disturbance.

"Does the church really fear an attack?" I asked, rolling over to look at him.

"We have received many threats through the years," John answered. "And occasionally a visitor to worship will begin making anti-gay statements. Nothing too serious has ever transpired, but of course we take precautions."

Then, John squeezed me tighter and said, "I worry about you and your congregation. You have none of the safeguards we do, and Oklahoma is even scarier than Dallas."

"I don't think our congregation has ever had an incident," I said, trying to assure him. "We are so much smaller, most people don't even know about us. You all are big and in the news a lot."

"But," he said, turning my head so he could look me in the eyes, "if you do your job well, that will change. People will know about you, and that could draw unwanted attention."

Then, he added, "I fear for you personally. What if you are attacked? What if someone tries to kill you? You are already pretty public, and there are lots of crazy people."

I touched his cheek. "I'm not sure why, but I'm not worried about that. I'm not afraid. I really don't think that anything is going to happen, but if something does and I'm harmed, then it's not like my worrying about it would have helped."

We silently spooned as I pondered the conversation. Then, I realized something for the first time and turned to look at him again.

"You know, I'm not afraid, because if something were to happen to me, it could probably be used for good. I'm willing to be a martyr for my faith and for something I believe in, if that's what happens. I'm not going to seek it out, but it doesn't frighten me."

"It frightens me," he said before grabbing me and kissing me repeatedly, a tear rolling down his cheek.

19

New In Town

"You have great hair. I like the curls. And that gap between your front teeth. It's very compelling." He was a tall, well-dressed guy with his own head of dark wavy hair. I was at a mixer hosted by the Diversity Business Association. Being new in Oklahoma City, I took every opportunity to meet new people so I could make friends and evangelize for the church.

"Thanks," I said to Mr. Slick, who said he was intrigued that I was a pastor.

"Are you seeing anyone?" he asked.

I almost started laughing at how direct this guy was. "Yes, I do have a boyfriend. He lives in Dallas."

He cocked his head and stared at me a moment before asking his next question. "Why are you dating someone long distance?"

These questions were unsettling me, but I didn't walk away. "I used to live there," I answered. "Plus, I'm there for work most weeks. We met, there was chemistry, and now we are dating." I wasn't sure I needed to explain myself, but hoped this answer would suffice.

But Mr. Slick didn't quit. "Is it serious?"

I answered honestly. "Not really, not yet. We've only been together a few months."

He was still looking intently at me. "Here's a scenario," he said. "If we were dating, and I called you up on Tuesday and said 'Let's go away for the weekend to a cabin in the mountains,' would you do that? Would you be spontaneous, drop everything, and go?"

I was thinking, *Boy, this guy comes on strong.* But I was also enjoying the attention.

"That sounds like fun," I said, smiling. "But I usually can't drop everything and go away for the weekend, since I preach on Sundays."

He furrowed his brow. "That would be a problem," he said, and glanced around the room.

But he still asked for my phone number before he left that night. Later that week, he called to set up dinner.

"You realize I'm seeing someone," I said. "I'm not going to go on a date with you."

"I'm interested in getting to know you," he said. "Plus, I want to know more about your church. It will be a work dinner, okay?"

I agreed. And then wondered if I was flirting with temptation.

Over coffee in the breakfast nook the next morning, I told my Mom about the impending dinner.

"Well, you are meeting lots of new people," she said. Then she looked up from the newspaper she was reading. "Maybe you shouldn't be in a steady relationship right now, especially a long-distance one?"

That wasn't the response I expected. "Even if that's true," I responded, avoiding the possible implications of her comment, "I don't think I want to date this guy. He's too slick."

"I know what you mean," she said taking a sip of coffee and looking back down at the paper. "But you're enjoying someone flirting with you."

At dinner, Mr. Slick wore a well-tailored suit and a starched white shirt with silver cuff links. By comparison, I was rather casually dressed in jeans. He explained that he worked on the business side of a television station, which required the fancy duds.

I did my best to ignore the secret thrill I felt when he invited me back to his place after dinner. *It's just because I'm enjoying the conversation*, I told myself. For the record, we had talked a lot about religion, faith, and my church. Hurricane Katrina had struck earlier that week, and he shared about how awful the video was that was coming into the TV station.

"The stuff we aren't broadcasting," he added.

Mr. Slick lived alone in a big suburban house. After giving me a tour, he told me to open our beers while he went and changed into jeans and a t-shirt. We sat out on the back porch and drank. He began this phase of the conversation by telling me that I should dump the boyfriend.

"Well, I love him," I said. "He's caring and fun." And I began to wonder how this evening was going to end. More precisely, I wondered how I *wanted* the evening to end.

He leaned back in his chair and slowly sipped his beer. "But you could have even more fun—traveling, expensive dinners, et cetera."

I told him that I liked what John and I shared. But he was probably wondering what I was doing at his house, having this conversation, if my relationship with John was so great.

We began to chat about other things, and I decided that

when I finished my beer I'd excuse myself and leave. I knew I might be giving up the chance for a fun night, but I didn't want to be the kind of guy who would cheat. This was the first time I had been seriously tempted, and I had come very close. Too close.

When I stood up to leave, Mr. Slick was clearly disappointed. He never called again. Oh, and he never did visit the church.

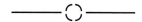

In the late summer, Second John began acting differently. He wasn't as joking and playful. He wasn't taking me out for nice dinners anymore or giving me surprise bouquets of flowers. He hadn't visited me in Oklahoma City. And as my obligations to my new church and community increased, I wasn't in Dallas quite as much as I had been.

That September, I finally called him to express my concerns. He said he was stressed out and anxious about work stuff. He acknowledged that maybe he was even depressed.

A week or so later, I was back in Dallas for work, and we met for dinner at the Black-Eyed Pea on Cedar Springs. Paul and Jason joined us. After dinner, John walked me to my car in the parking lot behind the restaurant. I went to open my car door saying that I'd meet him at his condo, when he took me by the hand.

I turned to face him, and John, suddenly looking very serious, said, "Scott, I don't think you should come over and spend the night tonight."

"What?" I exclaimed, dropping his hand. "Why?"

He took a deep breath and said, quite calmly, "In fact, I don't think you should come over anymore at all. I don't think this relationship is working out for either of us."

I took a moment to compose myself. "John, let's not talk about this in the parking lot behind the Black-Eyed Pea. Please?" I begged. "Can we go to your place and have a conversation?"

He looked down at the pavement, hesitating before answering. "Fine," as he turned to walk to his car. But then he spun around and added, "But don't bring your luggage in."

Back at his condo he explained all the reasons he didn't think the relationship was working. The distance was a problem. He was worried I was still in love with First John. He knew I was meeting guys in Oklahoma City. He thought I needed to explore being out and having more experience.

What he said didn't make sense to me. I had an argument for everything he said. When he finished talking, I contemplated three responses.

First, I could simply get up from the couch, say "Goodbye," and walk out. This response had the simplicity of resolving my own recent ambivalence about the relationship while appearing strong and dignified.

Or I could ignore everything he said and simply get up from the couch, walk into his bedroom, strip, and crawl under the sheets. Response Number Two seemed daring, sexy, and fun. And given how horny John usually was, it might just work.

The third possibility was to argue for why I thought he was wrong.

I chose Number Three, of course. I'm too much a creature of habit. And of course Number Three didn't get anywhere.

None of my arguments persuaded him, and when I finally left, I felt pathetic.

Then I drove across the city to my now mostly empty house, devoid of all the things that once made it feel like home, and crawled into my bed alone, angry at John, and disappointed at myself.

That weekend I traveled to Austin with a few friends to attend the Austin City Limits Music Festival. We had some trouble getting away that Friday, as supplies like bottled water were difficult to find. Hurricane Rita was set to make landfall on the Gulf Coast sometime that week. With the memory of Katrina still fresh in their minds, Dallasites were freaked out and preparing for the apocalypse. I wasn't sure why people hundreds of miles from the coast thought their water supply would be wiped out, but they apparently did, as every grocery store's bottled water aisle was empty. I couldn't understand why people were fleeing the hill country of central Texas, either, but our car was one of the few heading south on I-35. The north-bound lanes were packed solid.

No storms affected the festival that weekend. Instead, we had roasting heat. I brought the dorky straw cowboy hat I'd worn to summer camp the year before. I was no longer worried that wearing it might make me look gay. I applied copious amounts of sunscreen and tied a red bandanna around my neck. Most importantly, I brought along a bright red umbrella to cast some shade to sit in.

Listening to the bands, I had plenty of time to think and sort through everything with John. Our relationship had been so much fun at first. And I had learned a lot from him, both personally and professionally. It had been a good relationship for newly out me. But even I had experienced doubts as John's mood had changed and I'd met new and interesting guys in Oklahoma City. Plus, there were the hints that Mom had dropped into conversations suggesting that I explore being single. I began to wonder if breaking up was for the best, even if I thought John's reasons for it were stupid.

Listening to Buddy Guy perform made me horny. When he proclaimed, "You are goddamned right I've got the blues," I yelled out, "Fuck yeah!"

The dry grass of Zilker Park was trampled by a hundred thousand pairs of feet that weekend, and by day three, the dust was so intense we were all covering our noses and mouths with wet bandannas, squirting copious amounts of Visene into our eyes, and popping cough drops like they were the latest fad drug.

The closing set was Coldplay. The hottest band in the world at that time, they had grown from having a small fan base of music snobs to dominating mainstream radio. My group of friends were all looking forward to seeing them for the first time. But the dusty haze was so intense, we could barely see the stage. After only a few songs, red-eyed Joel turned to the rest of us and said, "Can we leave? I feel miserable." We all agreed and began to trudge back to our car.

That autumn, our church supported the exhibition of a traveling show from the Smithsonian Institution on the treatment of homosexuals in the Holocaust. The initiative was organized by the Cimarron Alliance Foundation, a local Oklahoma City organization focused on LGBT equality, mostly through public education events like this one. The board was composed of what are often called "A Gays"—the lawyers, doctors, businesspersons, and other gay people of means and connections. Oklahoma City was fortunate to have a class of such people who were deeply committed to the cause of LGBT rights.

A few months before the show opened, I was contacted by Rob Howard, the person from Cimarron who was doing most of the legwork drawing in community partners for the exhibit. He wanted to meet for coffee at Panera Bread and discuss how the church could support the initiative.

Rob was in his late fifties, with short, pale hair and a fair complexion. He rose as I entered the café. "I'm also looking forward to getting to know you a little better," he said as we shook hands. "So let's talk about the exhibit, and then we can simply chat."

Once I'd returned with my coffee and joined him at the table, Rob explained the purpose of the exhibit.

"Because Oklahoma has such vocal anti-gay politics, we want to educate the public on what the extreme edge of anti-gay politics really looks like," he said. I was excited by what he told me about the exhibit and agreed that the church would support it.

Then we started sharing our own individual stories. Rob was a retired Northwest Airlines executive. He had grown up in Oklahoma City and was raised a Southern Baptist. We discovered that his childhood pastor had been my pastor during my freshman year of college. Rob had served in the military, married a woman, and had a son.

After he came out in the early 1980s, he and his wife amicably divorced and remained friends. They continued to co-parent along with Art, Rob's partner of twenty-five years. Rob and Art had also helped to found a church in Minneapolis. They moved back to Oklahoma City in the early 2000s when Rob retired. They came seeking warmer weather and to care for Rob's elderly mother, who died not long after.

Rob's passion was advocating for LGBT seniors. He told me that many seniors have to re-enter the closet when they move into assisted living or nursing homes, as those facilities often have minimal or no training or services for LGBT persons. In fact, senior care facilities can be locations of abuse and discrimination toward LGBT persons. I had previously been unaware of this issue.

Rob and I spent more than an hour chatting. We enjoyed each other so much that we began meeting for lunch about once a month. Rob was one of those people who liked to stay connected to the entire LGBT community. One way he did that was nurturing relationships with a wide variety of people.

Within a couple of months we realized we really enjoyed one another and that we worked very well together. We were becoming good friends.

"You sure are hanging out with Rob a lot," Mom said one afternoon. We were in the garden behind her house, where I was helping her weed the flower beds.

"He's my best friend," I said. I hadn't thought that before, but the words sounded right when I said them.

"Really? But he's thirty years older than you," she said. "He's my age, actually."

"I know. That doesn't seem to matter."

Not long after that, I told Rob about the conversation with my mother, somewhat nervous to be sharing the news that I thought he was my best friend. *Would I sound like a silly schoolgirl?*

Rob laughed and said, "Funny you say that, because I've been thinking about that lately as well. You are my best friend in Oklahoma City."

The Holocaust exhibit opened with a big reception. My parents accompanied me to the gallery in the newly fashionable old warehouse district of the city. The bare brick walls and exposed pipes provided an appropriate setting for the images of pain and suffering on display.

Leaders of the Oklahoma City gay and Jewish communities mingled with one another while sipping from clear plastic cups of wine. I was able to introduce my parents to many of my new friends and acquaintances, including Rob.

The publisher of a local LGBT news site, *Hard News Online,* approached me. "Have you ever considered writing a column?" he said. "We'd like you to think about writing for us."

I hadn't thought about it, but I immediately knew I'd enjoy it, and I told him so. He said he'd call me soon so we could discuss the details.

"That will be fun," said Mom as he walked away. "What an honor."

I'd noticed one of the servers looking at me like he recognized me. I couldn't place how we knew each other. The next time I went up for a drink, he addressed me by name.

"Scott, what would you like?" As he refilled my cup with red wine, he asked, "You don't remember me, do you?"

I shook my head. "You look very familiar, but I can't place you."

"Oklahoma Baptist University. I was a year behind you. My name is Kevin."

It took me a minute to remember, but finally it clicked. "Yes, of course," I answered with enthusiasm. "I do remember you. How are you?" We chatted for a while. He told me he'd been following my work.

"You're doing a great job," he said.

I thanked him. Before I left that night, he gave me his number.

The next week I went to Office Depot and found a little black book for keeping phone numbers.

20

"I'll take it."

I spent Thanksgiving weekend in a log cabin near Beaver's Bend State Park with my parents, who had planned the trip for the trout fishing. After a particularly chilly morning sitting on a rock beside the river, I had concluded that trout fishing in November was simply not my thing. But I didn't have the heart to tell my parents.

One afternoon my cell phone beeped, indicating that I had a voicemail and also, at least momentarily, a signal. Reception was spotty in the pine woods of southeastern Oklahoma.

I pushed play on my voicemail and perked up when I recognized the voice of my real estate agent in Dallas. I finally had an offer on my house. So in December, all those months of sometimes-awkward crashing with my parents finally came to an end.

Because of the reduced income of my new job, I decided to rent, but the prospect of apartment hunting didn't excite me. I was driving around near the Paseo Arts District—a fun, colorful neighborhood of old bungalows and 1930s apartment buildings with galleries, bars, jewelry shops, and hip restaurants, when I passed a for rent sign in the yard of a rather nice-looking brick house. I circled around again to get a better look at the place.

The two-story house with light brown brick and lots of windows sat on a corner with a slight slope up to the front. The unit for rent was the bottom floor of the house, and it contained much space for entertaining and many unique architectural details. The living room was long and wide, with a big arch opening into the dining room that was large enough for my pool table. There were arched French doors leading into the delightful sunroom. The breakfast nook contained lovely built-in cabinets with glass doors. The crown molding throughout was more than twelve inches tall. The floors were a beautiful hardwood, and the fireplace was covered with custom ceramic tiles with images of the Sierra Nevadas and Sequoia trees.

The landlady was only asking $750 a month. When we signed the contract, she told me, "I have the sense that you are the right person. I like the idea of having a minister here."

I moved the week of Christmas. Bob, the church's music director, rode with me down to Dallas, where I rented a U-Haul and recruited a bunch of my former youth and some other friends to help us load up. Snow was falling when we arrived back in Oklahoma City. Around twenty church members and new friends assisted with the unloading. One older guy who couldn't lift brought soup. Another couple brought a big laundry basket full of cleaning supplies. The lesbians took over anytime something heavy needed to be hauled, which made my mom laugh.

The church was thriving. In August we had celebrated the

Oklahoma City congregation's fifth anniversary with 150 people in attendance, the largest attendance in years. Membership and giving were up. I had recruited new leadership, including Paula Sophia, who helped coordinate our social activism as a volunteer Minister of Justice and Peace. We launched a new small group in Norman that we hoped might become a model for other small groups around the region.

The big annual service project was giving baskets at Christmas to people living with HIV/AIDS. The baskets were filled with toiletries, cleaning supplies, and candy. In order to raise money for the project, the church hosted an annual dinner at which we auctioned off centerpieces created by church members. They varied from formal and elegant to small and whimsical. That year the dinner and auction raised thousands of dollars, setting a record.

The congregation also gave me a great gift for Christmas— a variety of vestments (albs, chasubles, and stoles) which they had purchased from two retired ministers.

One Sunday we were visited by a family whose teenage daughter had a severe developmental disability. She was unable to speak, but had a big smile and kept hugging everyone. The family came forward together to receive communion. After worship, her parents told me this was the first time their daughter had ever taken communion. They explained that in the church they previously attended, it was denied her. The minister of that congregation told her parents that in order to receive communion a person had to stand before the congregation and make a profession of faith.

"My daughter cannot speak," the girl's mother said to the

minister. "Are you telling me that because she cannot speak, she is not in the kingdom of God?"

In an email I received after the worship service, the girl's father wrote, *When we visited your church, we heard you say that the table was open to all— we were all invited—and we took that to mean that she could take communion. Of all God's children she, I believe is so full of love. … Thank you for opening your doors to us.*

I was so excited to finally be in my own place that December. In two weeks I completely unpacked, decorated—including Christmas decorations—and hosted a big New Year's Eve party.

Brokeback Mountain opened in Oklahoma City that January. *Hard News Online*, the news site I was now writing for, hosted a sold-out showing at the local AMC. Standing in line waiting for the theatre to open, I was excited to see such a crowd—elderly lesbians, queer teens, middle-aged gay couples, and more. We were thrilled that a gay film was a major release with serious Oscar buzz. We were also thrilled that rural gays were being portrayed. Some of us were hot for Heath Ledger and/or Jake Gyllenhaal. As other moviegoers passed our line, you could see their confusion as they looked at the excited crowd of queers.

Energized by the film, and even a little horny, I went out to one of the gay bars afterwards, where I ran into a guy named Greg. He was there with friends, and invited me to join them at their table. Let me tell you about Greg.

We had met over Labor Day weekend dancing at the Copa. He was a little shorter than me, with dark hair, a goatee, and piercing eyes. I thought he was the most attractive guy I'd seen in Oklahoma City, so imagine my joy when he called me for a date. But, the day following the date, he called to say he just wanted to be friends.

Fast forward to January, and I hadn't gotten over my attraction to Greg. We ended up leaving the bar at the same time, and I asked him, "Do you want to see my new place?"

He hesitated a moment before answering, "Sure." Then he added, "But we aren't going to sleep together."

As I gave him a tour of the house, he commented on its various unique architectural features. I had purposely begun the tour in the kitchen, and circled around the house, saving the bedroom for last.

He grinned as we entered. "I said we aren't going to sleep together."

"I know," I said turning to him with a grin.

Then he kissed me. And we slept together.

21

Soulforce Equality Ride

In the winter of 2006, Soulforce announced the Equality Ride. My alma mater, Oklahoma Baptist University, was on the schedule.

Soulforce is an organization that advocates for LGBT equality, in particular by addressing religious-based discrimination. It was founded by Mel White, who came to fame when he exited the closet after years working as a ghost writer for the likes of Jerry Falwell, Pat Roberston, and Billy Graham. He was as inside the right-wing Christian power structure as one could be. His memoir *Stranger at the Gate* was widely read in the LGBT community.

I had read the book the year before, during my first months of pastoring at Cathedral of Hope. In the early 1990s Mel had worked briefly as the dean of Cathedral of Hope Dallas. I was moved by his description of the church in the final chapter and its joyful worship that provided hope and healing.

Now Mel White's organization, Soulforce, would be coming to the area to advocate for LGBT equality at my alma mater. The Equality Ride was based upon the idea of the Freedom Rides which had been used in the struggle for integration in the Jim Crow South. These new rides would include LGBT young adults trained in nonviolent direct action in the Gandhi and King models. They would travel by bus to visit religious colleges and universities that had anti-gay policies on the books. Most of these were in the South. The hope was to engage the schools in dialogue about the issue. If dialogue was rejected, then the riders hoped to at least spend a day or two on each campus talking to students in the student union. They would make use of the internet to connect with students ahead of time, especially any LGBT students who might be on campus. If a university rejected both of these measures, then the riders would demonstrate against them, even to the point of getting arrested for trespassing.

Responses from universities were varied. Some set up panel discussions with the riders. Others banned them from coming on campus and tried to block the school's computer networks from accessing information about the ride. When the riders attempted to walk peacefully onto these campuses, they were arrested. Tulsa's Oral Roberts University was one of the places where this happened.

When Soulforce announced its plan to visit Oklahoma Baptist University, I volunteered to help. They invited me to speak at a press conference scheduled for the second day of activities. I also promised to be there the first day, when they would try to visit campus.

The university decided to welcome them. The school didn't organize a panel or any formal dialogue, but they did allow the riders to spend the day in the student union, the Geiger Center, talking with students.

I arrived ahead of the riders. I wore one of my old OBU sweaters, despite it being a bulky extra-large. Back in the 90s everyone wore bulky clothes, even tiny teenage girls. *Jeez*, I wondered, *Did I really wear this crap when I was younger and skinnier?*

Shortly after arriving in the Geiger Center, I ran into a few administrators I knew. They welcomed me and remarked on my almost-vintage sweatshirt, laughing at how big it was.

The day's events went well, with no disruptions. When the Riders arrived, I introduced myself to those I didn't know. Then I introduced the Riders to administrators and faculty. Throughout the day, I answered questions and joined in conversations with current OBU students. Many faculty who knew me were excited to see me, and we had pleasant talks catching up. A number of them remarked that they'd seen me in the news.

A student who had heard about the Equality Ride chose to come out before they arrived at OBU. Her name was Lauren, and her story appeared in *Newsweek* magazine the week the ride arrived in Oklahoma. Surprising to many of us alumni, the university did not kick her out of school. Nor did they require her to go through reparative counseling. A new day appeared to be dawning.

That night the Equality Riders hosted a public information session at a restaurant just two blocks from my house. I was chatting with Paula Sophia and her wife when I noticed the arrival of a very handsome young guy with black hair and an olive complexion. He was well dressed in an orange button-down shirt, nice-fitting jeans and a sport coat, and he carried himself with confidence and vitality.

A number of the Riders jumped up as he entered. "Michael!" I heard several of them say as they rushed to greet him.

Who is this guy? I wondered. With as much discretion as I could manage, I watched him expertly work the room as I ate. Eventually he came to our table and greeted Paula, who introduced him to me.

"This is Michael Cich," she said. "He's a student at Oklahoma State University and part of their gay-straight alliance, SODA." (The acronym stands for Sexual Orientation Diversity Alliance). "Michael's in charge of their annual conference, which is coming up in April. He's invited me to be the keynote speaker."

Paula introduced me, "This is our pastor, Scott. I believe you wanted to invite him to speak as part of the religious panel?"

I was thrilled when he smiled at me and said, "Nice to meet you. I hope that will work out?"

There was no question. I was definitely going to attend that conference!

I gave him my business card and hoped he'd linger to chat, but he moved on to the next table.

The Equality Riders held a press conference the next day. I was scheduled to speak after a young lesbian shared her story. I noticed Michael in the crowd.

The young woman had attended OBU in the early 2000s and was outed her sophomore year by someone she thought was a friend. The university segregated her, placing her in a dorm room all by herself on a floor that was otherwise empty of students. They also required that she attend counseling. Her parents reacted negatively to her. She eventually dropped out of the university, and what followed was depression and addiction. Only recently had she begun to recover.

As I got up to speak, I couldn't stop crying. I apologized for my tears and explained that I had been deeply pained by what she'd told us.

"This school nurtured me," I said, "but it hurt her." I admitted that I hadn't been out while I was a student, but that I had spoken against the anti-gay policy. I told the story of Sean Baugh's expulsion from the university.

Finally controlling my sobs, I shared how I had warned the university administration in 1993 that it had blood on its hands and that if it kept up with this policy, it was going to destroy someone's life.

"Today I've heard a story that confirms my worst fears," I said at the conclusion of my talk. "I warned them to no avail."

The one administrator who had chosen to attend the press conference looked stricken.

After the press conference, a handful of people stopped to greet me. Michael was one of them. He shook my hand and thanked me for what I'd shared.

"Your emotion was very touching," he said.

I responded, "I could barely talk."

"Because of that, you were very effective," he said. Once again, I hoped for a longer conversation, but he moved on to speak with someone else.

Later that week I heard from the OBU administrator who had attended the press conference. He said he wanted to talk with me, so we met for coffee in Oklahoma City. He asked for my story in more detail. He told me he had gone back to the university's files and read up on Sean Baugh, for he had not been privy to that information at the time of the events. He then inquired about other out alumni. He asked if I could contact some of them and ask them to share their stories with the school. I agreed.

I then asked something of him. The day the Equality Ride spent in the Geiger Center, some students had asked me to return and give a Bible study about homosexuality from my perspective. I asked if I would be allowed to meet with this group on campus. He said that of course I was allowed to be present on campus and talk with students, but that such a meeting couldn't be an official or advertised event. I said that was fine.

And, then, in a move that surprised me, he said the university leadership wanted to take steps to make things different. He asked me to agree to something. If I would keep it secret, they would refer struggling gay students to me. Of course I agreed.

"But if you ever acknowledge it publicly, the arrangement will end," he told me. "And we will deny it ever existed."

I said I understood.

I reveal this agreement now because more than a decade has passed. I haven't been living in Oklahoma City for many years, and nobody has been referred to me for a long time. Also, a new university administration seems to have turned back to a more homophobic approach.

In the place you call home, your ministry is different from every other place. You have history and relationships with more people. You speak the language. You know how things work and don't work.

After I returned to Oklahoma, I kept running into people from my past, people from the Baptist world who knew and respected me and were still trying to wrap their heads around my coming out. One day at a coffee shop I encountered the man who had been the Dean of Students at OBU a decade before—the man we had confronted about Sean Baugh's removal from the school. The former dean was now pastoring a church in Oklahoma City.

He walked directly over when he saw me. "Scott, so good to see you," he said. "I heard you were back in town." I invited him to sit, and he did. We chatted for about fifteen minutes, catching up on each other's families and our jobs.

As he rose to leave, he reached out his hand again. "Good to see you and catch up," he said.

"Same here," I responded, surprised by the kind and respectful encounter. Maybe things had changed even for him.

22

"How did he find out?"

Mom and her siblings had decided against telling Pappoo that I was gay. They thought he would be unaccepting due to his age and generation. None of them wanted to face that possibility and what impact it might have upon the family. My sister Erin disagreed with the family decision because she thought Pappoo had a right to know. I said I was willing to abide by the family decision for the time being, but when I had a reason for him to know, like a serious relationship, we'd have to revisit the issue.

When I moved back to Oklahoma City and became a public figure, the family was nervous that Pappoo might hear about me through the news. But because he lived three hours away with different local TV and a different newspaper, and because he didn't use the internet, they decided this was still unlikely.

One day, my mom received a phone call from her sister Karen.

"Dad just called me to ask if Scotty was gay," Karen told Mom. "I told him I didn't know anything. I said he'd have to talk to you."

"How did he find out?" Mom asked.

"He received a call from Aunt Lavenia. She asked him if Scotty was gay. She said that Charlotte had seen something about it on the internet."

"Those damn busybodies should have minded their own business," Mom said. She had always been a very private person with an unlisted phone number, and she hated how the internet had made information public.

Lavenia was Pappoo's older sister, and Marcia was one of her daughters. When I was a kid, Lavenia and her husband Art owned a beautiful home on the rocky shore of Grand Lake, where they hosted Fourth of July barbecues and other large family gatherings.

Uncle Art died when I was eighteen. He had been an atheist, the only one in the family. Lavenia asked me to do the funeral, which was my first. I visited a couple of other ministers to ask their advice.

The first one told me, "You have an audience that probably includes non-Christians, so you should take the opportunity to share the Gospel with them, offering them the opportunity to accept Jesus Christ as their Lord and Savior."

That didn't sound right to me. I was glad when the other minister I visited said something different.

"Don't do that," he said when I told him about the first advice I'd gotten. "Comfort the family and share stories of the deceased. In this case, everyone in your family knows your uncle was an atheist, so no need to draw any attention to that. Is his wife religious?"

I said she was, so he told me to comfort her with her religious faith.

That's what I tried to do, mostly sharing stories of Uncle Art. Aunt Lavenia and his children seemed happy with the service. They even gave me a portfolio as a thank-you gift. *Rev. Scott*

Jones is inscribed on the cover, even though I wasn't ordained at that time. I still use it every Sunday morning to carry my sermon manuscript to the pulpit.

After the phone call from Karen, Mom called to tell me about it and ask what I thought we should do.

I sighed when she first told me that he knew. I was a little annoyed that I hadn't already told him myself, but I hoped this might give him some time to think about it before he and I sat down to talk. I told Mom I'd take off work the next day and drive to Miami.

"I don't want you to do this alone," Mom responded. "I'll take off work, too, and we can go together. If telling him doesn't go well—and it might not—you won't have to drive home alone, emotional."

No matter how the conversation went, I was sure I wouldn't be so devastated that I couldn't drive. But told her I appreciated it. And I did. Having Mom along would make the task easier.

She called to tell Pappoo that we were coming.

When we arrived, he didn't come outside to greet us like he usually did. Instead, we were greeted at the door by Sue, my step-grandmother.

"Why Sandra, Scott," she said. "I didn't know you were coming!" Apparently Sue's dementia was getting worse, I thought.

"Good to see you, Sue," I said as I hugged her. "We are here to talk to Grandpa. Mom called him last night to tell him we were coming."

"Then I'm sure he told me. I must have forgotten," she said. "Do you want something to drink? How about a Dr. Pepper? Are you hungry?" She escorted us into the family room that opened onto the kitchen. Pappoo was sitting on the faux red leather couch, watching a Western with the sound turned up loud.

"Hi Dad," Mom said as she walked over to him. He rose from the couch to hug her. "Sandra, Scotty." He nodded in my direction. "How was your drive?"

Mom told him the drive was fine, with only a little traffic in Tulsa.

I walked over to him and said, "I'm here to talk with you about Lavenia's phone call."

"I figured," he said, clicking off the TV. We all just stood there a moment, Sue smiling, the rest of us stony faced. "Why don't we go out to the sunroom," he said to me.

Mom remained with Sue in the family room as Pappoo and I walked toward the sunroom. As we passed through the dining room, I noticed a Bible on the table. Pappoo picked it up and carried it with him.

Pappoo had built the sunroom himself, converting what had been an open-air deck. The windows were slightly open, allowing us to hear the songs of birds in the backyard. I could see that his garden was doing well. The green beans would be ready soon. Benches lined the walls, and in good weather the entire family could eat a meal out here. We sat down and he leaned forward, putting the Bible and his elbows on the table.

I got directly to the point. "I am gay," I said. He grimaced slightly but didn't say anything, so I went on and told him some of the basics of my story, of how I'd wrestled with coming out, finally finding the courage and integrity to do so.

He listened attentively and took great care before speaking. I was relieved that he didn't get angry.

When he finally spoke, he was calm. "I don't understand it," he said in a gentle, caring tone. "The Bible is clear that homosexuality is a sin. And you are a minister. You have studied God's word. I know you know what the Bible says. That bothers me."

At this moment I didn't want to get into a debate over the interpretation of the Bible. Discussing the proper translation of Greek words or the historical and cultural contexts and biases of the authors didn't seem like the most helpful topics of conversation. But I needed to say something.

"Pappoo, what you've said is one perspective on the Bible, but it's not the only one. Many Christian thinkers, including entire denominations, don't think scripture condemns homosexuality. You know that I've studied all of this thoroughly."

"Yes, I know that," he gazed momentarily out the window before turning back to look at me. "I was always a little nervous of the things you studied in school. I didn't like that you studied philosophy instead of continuing to study the Bible."

I knew he'd had that concern. Yet I'd remained in the closet while I was studying philosophy. Only when I was working as a full-time minister had I found the confidence to come out.

"Pappoo, you know me. I'm the same person you've always known. I'm a good person, a faithful Christian, a serious person."

He took a deep breath and looked as if he was contemplating what I said. "Scotty," he called me by my childhood name as he leaned closer. "Sin infects all of us, even those determined to do right and be faithful." His voice was not stern. He did not speak in anger. He seemed disappointed but there was a hopeful sound in his tone.

I leaned closer too. "Pappoo, I don't believe being gay is sin. In fact, I've experienced great freedom since I came out. The Spirit of God is with me and my work. My church is reaching people, helping them, changing their lives for the better."

He glanced out the window again where some birds were feeding on the lawn. "Are there other gay people in your church?" he asked.

Glad the focus had shifted away from me, I nodded and told him that there were. "Our membership is mostly gays and lesbians. They are good, kind, caring people who are faithful Christians. They've been hurt by the churches they grew up in and have been struggling to reclaim their faith."

He had no immediate response. He seemed to be watching the birds.

When he turned back to look at me, there was a new earnestness in his voice. "Scotty, I love you, but I can't accept this. I think the Bible is clear. I think you have been tempted by sin and have fallen under its control. I pray for you to repent and find your way back to God."

I hung my head as he continued.

"When you were a child, we all knew that God had so much in store for you. There was such promise, and we were all excited when you became a minister. I still think God wants to use you to do great things. You must overcome this sin." He had placed his hand upon the Bible during this exhortation.

"Grandpa, God is using me," I said, hoping my voice conveyed my conviction and joy. "What I'm doing right now is my calling. I have never felt closer to God or closer to my calling since I had the integrity to finally be honest about who I am, who God made me to be. I know you don't understand that, but it is the truth."

I thought he might cry.

"I know that some men are more attracted to other men than they are to women," he said. "I met men like that when I was in the military, and I've known others through the years. So, it is possible that you are that type of man."

He opened his Bible to a bookmarked passage.

"I stayed up last night praying and reading the Bible, looking for answers that might help you. In 1 Corinthians 7, Paul writes about marriage and celibacy, and in the next chapter he talks about our bodies being the temple of God, that we have to dedicate our bodies to God and God's will for us. For instance, we read in verse thirty-two, 'I would like you to be free from concern. An unmarried man is concerned about the Lord's affairs—how he can please the Lord.'"

He looked directly at me as he continued. "Scotty, it may be that you are the kind of man who is attracted to other men. If this is true, then you must surrender your attractions to God. You should be celibate, so that God can use you to do the work that God wants you to do."

I realized then that this conversation had nowhere to go. He was hurt, and there was no way for me to assuage his pain. He was trying to be loving, to express the concern he felt for his grandson. But he was not hearing my story. His love was directed at his expectation of me, not the authentic me. My reality challenged the faith which had grounded and brought meaning to his life.

"Pappoo, I can't do that. Celibacy is not what God has

called me to. I'm not sure where our conversation can go at this point."

"Scotty, please hear me," he implored, clearly heartbroken.

"I do. Believe me, I do." And I stood. "Mom and I should get back on the road; the drive is long."

Yes, I was hurt by his rejection. But I wasn't angry or emotional. Instead, I chose in the moment not to let his response rob me of the joy and confidence I had developed since coming out. In fact, I pitied him for his inability to see me. I grieved that he would not experience the joy I had discovered.

I could only hope that over time his mind might slowly begin to change and that there would be further opportunities for dialogue. Maybe I'd give him "The Letter to Louise" so that he might begin to study and reflect on other interpretations. But that would wait for a later time. Before we could hurt each other anymore, this conversation must end.

As we walked back into the house, he placed the Bible back on the table.

Mom stood as we entered the den. She looked directly at me, and I gently shook my head. She turned toward Pappoo.

"Dad, I love my son," she said, staring at Pappoo as her voice was breaking. I noticed she was clenching her right fist as she added, "He is the person God made him to be. Don't hurt him." Then she relaxed her control, hung her head, and let the tears flow.

Pappoo stepped over and embraced Mom. She relaxed into him. As she continued to weep, tears began to trickle from under his eyeglasses. I watched this moment, proud of my mother but aware that because of me, her relationship with her father would now be forever altered.

Two weeks later my stepdad, Harold, called.

"Scott, I need you to come over right now," he said, sounding afraid. "Your mother is throwing a fit. I don't know what to do."

Caught off guard, I tried to understand. "Harold, what's happening?"

"Your Mom, she's really upset. She got some letters from someone, and she's crying and angry. It has something to do with you. Please come over." He was begging. I told him I'd be there as soon as I could.

When I arrived at their house, Harold met me at the door, worry furrowing his brow. He ushered me into the living room where Mom was curled up on the couch. The skin around her eyes was bright red. Her hair was a mess. From the look on her face, I couldn't tell if she was more hurt or angry.

She looked up when she saw me. "Those damn busybodies have ruined our family," she said.

I sat down beside her, took her hand, and asked who she was talking about.

"Marcia and Charlotte. They've hurt me as deeply as anyone ever could." Then she began to wail and shake. The only other time I'd ever seen her behave this was the day her mother died, when she had fallen to the living room floor and writhed, screaming and crying. That scene frightened me as a child, and now I was frightened again, wondering what had pained my Mom so. I stroked her arm and asked her to please back up and tell me what happened.

When she had regained some control she stared at me and

instead of answering my question said accusingly, "Why can't you be more private? Why does everything have to be so public? Why are you forcing the rest of us to take positions? Can't we just deal with all of this privately, as a family?"

I was stunned. *Where was this coming from?* She'd never given any hint that she felt this way. I was bewildered with how to respond. *Was this her distress talking, or were these her genuine feelings? Was Mom not as supportive as I had perceived her to be? All of this time was she simply putting a good face on the situation?* The fear of where this conversation might lead seized me. My mind ran through the possibilities. I worked to calm myself. I knew I had to proceed very carefully, speaking as comfortingly as I could.

"Mom, I don't know what you're talking about," I said. "I need you to tell me the story, so I can try to help."

"You can't do anything. You won't." She shook her head and wiped her face with a tissue.

"Please," I implored, growing more frightened with every second that she refused to talk.

Now she began a long cry that grew gentler with every slowly passing minute. She uncurled her body, sitting up on the couch. The entire time I held her hand and stroked her arm.

When her tears and sobs had finished, she sat in silence, wiping her face. Then, she turned toward me and spoke sternly.

"After we visited Pappoo, I decided to write Lavenia a letter in which I told her that she should have minded her own business. I told her that she had hurt the family and caused a rift. That we had decided not to tell Pappoo because we didn't want anything like this to happen."

I guessed that the letter was not well received.

Mom continued, "I wasn't mean. I wasn't cruel. But her kids were. Today I received two letters, one from Marcia and one from Charlotte, and they said such cruel things." She shook her head and the tears began again.

I didn't have to wait as long this time before she was composed again. Then I asked what they had said.

"They told me not to attack their mother. That she had every right to talk to her brother. And that if anyone was to blame for any division in the family, it would be you. And also me, for backing you."

"Okay," I said, thinking that didn't sound so bad, but expecting there must have been something more to cause her such anguish.

"But the letters were worse than that," Mom said, looking away from me as she continued. "They said awful, mean, cruel things about you. No mother should ever have to read such things about her son. And from family members," she exclaimed.

When I asked her what they said, she stared at me again, anger burning in her eyes. "I will never tell you. I tore the letters up."

I told her that I was sorry they had hurt her, that they had no grounds for attacking her for protecting her son. She wasn't comforted. The anger in her eyes continued to burn.

Mom clenched her jaw and raised her chin, "They said we had no right to keep the information from Dad, since you are all over the news and the internet. They said the information was public and that they were in their rights to talk about it."

On the one hand, they were right. My being a gay man was public information, and there was no way we could have ever kept the news from Pappoo forever. I didn't say that, because I knew those thoughts wouldn't comfort my mother, and I was still frightened of where this conversation was heading. Mom wasn't just hurt by these cruel letters; they had exposed a deeper pain which was directed at me.

Before tackling that deeper pain, I had one more thing to say about the letters. "They had no right to out me. They should have known that if Pappoo didn't know, there was a reason we had decided not to tell him."

She squeezed my hand back for the first time in this conversation, a reassuring gesture. My fear subsided, a little.

"Now they've ruined everything," she said, shaking her head. "Our family will never be the same."

I tried to assure her that wasn't true. "Give it time, and we'll see."

"I hope you are right." She leaned against my shoulder and I put my arm around her.

I took that intimate movement as a sign that I could broach her deeper pain. I was still afraid of where our conversation might end up, but I knew I had to address her concern. Staring straight ahead at the wall across the room, I began to talk.

"Mom, you know I have to be public. That's my job. My calling from God, even. Because I'm so public, I'm able to help other people. Hopefully I'm also helping to change the world."

Without looking at me, Mom put her hand on top of mine. "Yes, I know. I'm sorry."

Then she lifted her head from my shoulder, and we turned to face each other again. She drew up her shoulders, breathed deeply, and then spoke with great calm. The accusatory tone was gone, replaced by a mix of determination and love.

"But I don't think you understand what your decisions are costing the rest of us." I sighed and held back my own tears.

Mom continued, "My relationship with my daughter is damaged. Things may never be the same again with my father. Now I'll be forever separated from my extended family."

Her pain was overwhelming my self-control. A vortex of guilt and grief and sympathy swirled inexorably inside me, unrelenting, until I could no longer keep my tears at bay.

Mom reached out and took hold of my right hand. She fixed her gaze on the back of my hand, which she began to stroke.

Keeping her eyes on our hands, she expressed her deep pain. "But I feel like I must do all of this in order to keep my son. You need my love and support, but sometimes you ask too much."

Tears streaming down my cheeks, all I could mutter was a simple "I'm sorry." Then Mom hugged me against her, rubbing my back, as we cried together in silence.

23

Brazilian Independence Day

"Michael!" I almost shouted. "How are you? Where have you been all summer?"

Michael Cich looked at me with a confused expression, but after a few seconds he flashed me a smile that suggested he finally recognized me. Then he answered that he had just been working and taking classes.

I was excited to see this attractive man again after so many months, and began to enthusiastically share about my summer, including a trip to Florida where I spent a week just lying on the beach.

We were at a meeting of the Oklahoma City Pride Board of Directors in early August 2006. Rob Howard and I had decided that the Pride Festival and Parade needed to "step it up a notch," so we had recruited a few other friends and acquaintances to join us in running for election to the Pride Board.

The meeting ended around ten that night. Rob headed home, but I decided to go for a drink at The Boom with my friend Steven, who had also attended the meeting. I approached Michael and his friend Jack; together they had driven from Oklahoma State University in Stillwater.

With my biggest smile, I said, "We're going out for a drink. Do you two want to join us?"

And he said yes, they would meet us. *Was there a little sparkle in his eyes when he agreed?* I gave them directions and excitedly headed out with Steven for the bar.

About thirty minutes later, Michael and Jack still hadn't arrived. Steven and I assumed that we had been stood up. *Oh, well,* I thought. *Another rejection.*

Then they appeared, walking through the door of the bar. Michael had a sheepish look on his face, and Jack seemed a little annoyed. Michael explained that they had gotten lost and that Jack had simply wanted to give up and return to Stillwater. Michael insisted they follow through with the plans.

Laughing, he said, "I said to Jack, 'Two good-looking guys invited us for drinks, and we are going to meet up with them.'"

Steven and I each spent time chatting individually with both Jack and Michael. Jack was a philosophy major. He had also spent time in a Buddhist monastery in Taiwan. Michael was an advertising and marketing major who also worked for the university. He had grown up in an Oklahoma City suburb. After he learned about my philosophy background, he just assumed I would be into Jack.

I wasn't.

A couple of days later, I called Michael to see when he would next be in town. He told me he'd be back that Saturday. I invited him to meet me for coffee at the Red Cup, a great place full of old hippies, liberal Christian ministers, Jewish rabbis, and alterna-kids.

Michael arrived at The Red Cup in a nice dress shirt, cuff

links, and jeans. He ordered hot chocolate and explained that he didn't like coffee. I apologized for picking a coffee shop, but he smiled and said it was okay.

We sat outside under the canopy. Earlier in the day it had rained, but now the sun was out and the air was fresh and cool. That day I learned that Michael's dream was to go to film school in New York, that he had an identical twin brother who was straight, that his mother was an immigrant from the Philippines, and that his dad was a Navy veteran.

He asked about my work. He'd grown up Catholic, but had renounced the church as a teenager, never having been confirmed. Although he had never been personally religious, he said he wasn't turned off by religion. In fact, he said he appreciated the role it plays in other people's lives and how church creates community. So, that didn't sound discouraging.

Standing in the parking lot as we were about to leave, I realized he was preparing to hug me when a big dog appeared from behind the car next to us and happily leaped up onto Michael, leaving muddy, wet paw prints on his nice dress shirt. Michael laughed at the random, awkward moment, then reached out his hand for me to shake, instead of hugging me with his now muddy, wet shirt.

He called that Wednesday afternoon. "I'm in town today for work and wondered if you wanted to hang out this afternoon. I was thinking of going to the art museum; you could join me."

I eagerly said I would. And since that day, I've always recommended visiting an art museum on an early date. You talk, but not lots. You move around, occasionally wandering away from one another before drawing close again. You learn a lot about the other person's tastes. Plus you can laugh, as we did at the Oklahoma City Museum of Art's overabundance of Chihuly sculptures.

He came back to town for dinner the next evening. We met at a Brazilian place I'd told him about. When we arrived at Café Do Brazil, the long room was filled with what appeared to be rows of actual Brazilians in a loud and festive mood. The barrel vault was festooned with yellow and green, and a band was playing at full volume.

"Today's Brazilian Independence Day!" the hostess cheered when she greeted us. We ordered caipirinhas and examined the special holiday menu. We had difficulty hearing each other at times, but we enjoyed the party.

When I walked him to his car after dinner, that moment arrived when we knew we were going to kiss. We were standing close to one another, smiling, eager anticipation sparkling in our eyes. Just as I was about to lean in and brush his lips with mine, I noticed a security guard walking through the parking lot near where we stood. I paused inches away from Michael's face, and we both held our breaths. Unfortunately, the security guard paused also. I remember thinking, *Is he ever going to move on?*

Michael and I stood there awkwardly for a few seconds, leaning toward one another, our faces very close. Our grins grew broader, turning at first into giggles and then into wholehearted laughter. All the first-kiss tension melted away.

Finally, the security guard turned away and walked to the other side of the parking lot. My lips touched Michael's, and we giggled through our first kiss.

Mom was recovering from a recent hip surgery at Thanksgiving, so I hosted dinner at my house for around twenty friends and family members. I was in the middle of that final fifteen-minute rush when the guests began arriving and poking their heads into the kitchen to ask if they could help.

"Thirty minutes ago you could have," was what I wanted to say each time. But I just said no. At that point it was just easier to do the final tasks myself.

My sister Erin entered through the kitchen door with her husband, Adam, who carried their dishes to the serving table. Our relationship had finally begun returning to normal, a change in attitude I thought might be due to her pregnancy. Maybe she wanted her family close as she prepared to have her first child?

Her pregnancy was just beginning to show, I noticed as she walked over and hugged me. Then, without asking if I needed help, she grabbed a spoon and began transferring food from pots to serving dishes. Michael was helping, too, primarily by running dishes out to the serving table. Erin turned toward him as he came into the kitchen.

"Hi. I'm Erin," she said, extending a hand and flashing a big smile. "You must be Michael."

Despite the promising turn in our relationship, the energy in her voice was more than I expected. There were probably a couple of extra drops of sweat on my brow as I kept working, trying not to be obvious that I was spying on their exchange.

"I am. Nice to meet you," Michael said, shaking her hand. I wondered if his smile covered any feelings of surprise.

Later that night, as we lay in bed, I asked Michael how he thought meeting Erin had gone.

"It was fine," he said. He turned toward me and stroked my cheek. "Maybe that period of fighting is over."

"Maybe. I hope so," I said, leaning over to kiss him.

I had decided to take Michael home to the extended family Christmas at Pappoo's house. I remembered that Christmas drive in 2003 when I worried I might never return home for the holidays. I wasn't going to let that fear catch up with me now, after all I'd been through since then.

Of course, given the experience with Pappoo that summer, I wasn't sure what the reaction would be.

A week after Thanksgiving, Michael and I were cuddling on the couch when Michael confessed that he was nervous about going to Pappoo's house and being around my family. With a firmness of tone, he then added, "You need to know that I'm not going to let your grandpa or anyone else say anything bigoted around me. That's simply unacceptable, and I will say something."

"Yeah, I know you well enough already to understand that."

"Good," he said in response and went back to watching TV.

"But there is one thing," I said, and Michael looked down at me again, frowning slightly. "He might try to witness to you. He might give you a religious tract."

Michael laughed. "That will simply be funny."

"I'm glad you think so," I said.

I met Michael's family one Sunday over lunch at County Line Barbecue. They served heaping portions of meat covered with a sweet sauce. I was later to learn that grilled meat was never in short supply in the Cich household.

Jerry, his dad, had grown up in Minnesota in a Catholic family of Polish-German extraction. He had met Michael's mom, Ninfa, while serving in the Navy in the Philippines. It took Jerry three years to persuade her to come to America and get married.

Michael's older brother Allan and his wife Jewel were also veterans. She was also Filipino, but they had met when Allan was stationed in Italy. Michael's identical twin, Robert, was into computers and all things tech. He also liked tinkering with cars. Regina was the little sister, a high school student, with long black hair and a sassy attitude.

The Ciches all greeted me warmly and expressed their surprise that Michael was dating a minister.

After the lunch, Michael informed me that his mother had said she liked me. I was genuinely excited, as I really liked Michael and wanted this relationship to develop.

Michael then said, "Mom's never said that before about any of the guys I've dated."

"Oh, really?" I asked with even greater excitement. "That's something, then, isn't it?"

He laughed. "Must be," he said, and kissed me.

Michael came out to his family his sophomore year in college. He invited them all up to Stillwater for the day. Late in the evening when they were about to depart, he finally told them he was gay.

His mom turned to everyone in the room and asked them how they felt and, in turn, each person gave a supportive response. Then, when his dad's turn came, Jerry leaned forward and said, "I was worried for a moment there that you were going to say you were a Republican."

I was envious of how easily Michael's coming out had gone.

As Christmas neared, my uncles got into a disagreement that seemed destined to affect my family's celebration. Emails to the entire family were flying back and forth.

Two weeks before Christmas, the argument still wasn't resolved. After all these years I finally had someone to bring home for Christmas, and it appeared the event would be unpleasant.

"Maybe the argument between your uncles will be a distraction from you bringing your gay boyfriend?" Michael asked, trying to reassure me.

As we were discussing the situation, I had an epiphany. As much as I had always enjoyed family Christmas and looked forward to the day I would finally have a date to bring home, I simply didn't feel an obligation to my family anymore. We already planned to do Christmas Eve with Mom and Erin, and then spend Christmas Day with the Ciches. Why spend the weekend before at my extended family gathering?

"Holidays are supposed to be fun, so let's just avoid all the unpleasantness," I said. "Why don't we do something else?"

The Wootens would be hosting their annual Christmas party in Dallas that weekend, a notorious gathering known as the "Drunken-Carol-Sing-a-Long." Plus, Royal Lane would be performing Handel's Messiah. I proposed a trip to Dallas instead of my family Christmas, because it would be more fun.

Michael agreed to the plan and I emailed my family, telling them that since it didn't look like Christmas was going to be much fun, Michael and I were going to skip it and go to Dallas for the weekend.

My uncle Harley replied: "It's Christmas. You don't show up because it's fun. You have an obligation to your family."

Michael and I took the response as an ironic vindication of our decision.

Pappoo didn't use email, so I sent him a card expressing our regrets and explaining why Michael and I wouldn't be there. I would have preferred to call, but he'd become so hard of hearing it was difficult to talk to him on the phone.

A few days later, a letter arrived from Pappoo. I didn't want to read it. I left the envelope unopened.

When Michael arrived from Stillwater to spend the night, I handed the envelope to him and said nervously, "Can you open it and read the letter to me?"

"Why?" he asked rather confused. "Do you think it's going to be bad?"

"Yeah, I just have a sense that it is."

With reservations, he agreed. Michael broke the seal and lifted out a single sheet of yellow legal pad paper, covered with a handwritten letter. Then he started crying, dropped the paper, and walked out of the room.

I grabbed the sheet. Scrawled across the top in all caps were the words *Who's Michael? I don't want to know him.*

The rest of the page was filled with quotes from what we call the "clobber passages"—the six Bible verses fundamentalists use in their efforts to prove that God hates us.

I found Michael lying on the bed in the dark bedroom. I entered and curled up beside him. He pulled away.

"Why did you make me read that hatefulness?" he asked without looking at me.

"I'm so, so sorry. Please forgive me," I implored. "I had no idea he would attack you."

"That's cruel and evil," he spat out the words. "Why would anyone write something like that? Especially to his grandson?" Righteous indignation mixed with his pain.

"I don't know," I honestly answered, gently touching his side before adding, "That's not the grandfather I grew up with. He was always a kind and moderate man."

Michael did not find my comment comforting. He pulled away again.

I continued, "Even last summer when he and I talked, he wasn't mean like this. He rejected what I told him, but he wasn't cruel." Shaking my head I added, "I didn't expect this."

After a few minutes, Michael turned around to face me. He then reached out and laid his hand flat upon my cheek. "I left the church years ago because of its hateful treatment of gay people," he began. "My own family has always embraced and supported me. I don't have anything to do with people who speak to me in this way or treat me like this. I'm not going to start doing it now, not even for you."

I knew this was a decisive moment. I didn't hear Michael's words as a threat to end our relationship; his hand upon my cheek was an obvious sign of intimacy. But I would have to clearly state my priority.

And so I told him that I understood what he was saying and

that I would never ask him to endure the bigotry of my family.

Michael took a deep breath, withdrew the hand from my check and propped himself up on the pillow.

"Your grandfather doesn't want to know me," he stated matter-of-factly. "Well, I don't want to know him, either. That's easily done."

The emotion of the moment overcame me, as I realized fully how my life had changed. My hopes to maintain my relationship with my family were crushed. If I was going to love this man, then I had to break with Pappoo. I softly wept as I began to stroke Michael's cheek.

"If you are not welcome, then I'm not welcome," I said. "We go together. Until he changes his mind, I won't return, even if that means I never have Christmas or any other holiday with my family again."

"Now hold me," he said, and we lay there 'til we fell asleep in our clothes.

The next day I told Mom what had happened. She called back a few hours later to tell me that she had written a letter to Pappoo telling him what he wrote to me was wrong and cruel. She informed Pappoo she wouldn't be going home for Christmas either, nor any other holiday, as long as I didn't feel welcome in his home.

I told her she didn't need to do that, and she responded that she did, because she was my mother. Then she added, "And no one, not even my own father, can treat you that way."

Michael and I had a great time in Dallas, by the way.

24

Sally Kern

"Scott, would you like to comment on Rep. Sally Kern's anti-gay YouTube video?"

I was on the phone with a reporter friend of mine who worked at a local television station. I had been busy putting together the final touches on the Sexuality and Spirituality conference that would begin that evening.

I didn't know what he was talking about. I told him I'd been busy with the conference all day and hadn't seen the news.

The reporter responded that the station would definitely have cameras at the conference in order to get people's responses to this story. "Let me send you the link," he said. "Watch it and call me back if you want to comment."

He added, "And believe me, you'll have plenty of comments. Just call me when you've figured out which one you want on the local news."

I laughed and agreed.

Our conference had already received some press coverage because of public criticism from an evangelical pastor and former pro football player, Paul Blair, who was organizing a protest. The aim of the conference, which was sponsored by seven local churches, was to educate people on interpretations of the Bible that differ from those espoused by anti-gay conservative evangelicals like Blair and his followers.

We organizers had also received a potentially scary email which was initially circulated among our opponents by Blair. It suggested that the Minutemen, a right-wing militia, were going to show up for the protest.

Five months before, in the early autumn of 2007, a gay man who was an active member of the First Presbyterian Church was carjacked on the Strip. His body was later discovered in the wreck of his burned-out car. It showed signs of brutal torture. Law enforcement identified the killers as members of the Aryan Brotherhood. The murder was part of an initiation rite.

After that incident, Paul Thompson, Rob Howard, and I organized a vigil. We gathered under the lone tree on The Strip because it was adjacent to the largest parking lot. Scores of people poured out of the bars and clubs. I distributed the Christmas Eve candles from church. We began passing the flame as we mourned. People huddled together to protect their candles from the wind. One speaker announced that we were reclaiming our public space. Others called for the crowd to commit to changing Oklahoma's hate crimes laws so that they protected LGBT people. No one said what we were all thinking—that any of us could have been the dead man.

After the email about the militia's possible protest of our conference, an emergency meeting of the organizing clergy was called. Refreshingly, none of us felt genuinely threatened. Mark, a Unitarian pastor, pointed out that the KKK had threatened to show up at the last conference.

"But they never materialized," he reminded the group.

"Given the recent murder, I think we should at least be cautious," said Jonalu, another Unitarian. "The environment just seems different this year. The opposition is more outspoken."

Kathy, a UCC pastor, added "My worry is that people's fears and anxieties about the security situation will translate into low attendance."

The event was being hosted at a local university because their gay-straight alliance was co-sponsoring. The faculty advisor, David, was also present at the meeting. He assured us that the university had taken steps to ensure a safe event.

"Campus security has been notified, and they will be prepared," he said.

So when the reporter called me that afternoon, I initially thought he was calling about this security fear. *What now?* I wondered as I clicked on the YouTube link he had sent me.

The video was not one that Rep. Kern had released herself. Rather, someone had taped her while she was speaking to a small Republican gathering. The focus of the speech had been the perils of the gay community's political activities. Here is the section of the speech that elicited a public outcry:

> "What they're trying to do is send a message of intimidation to those people who are taking a stand for traditional marriage and against the homosexual lifestyle. They want to silence us, is what they want to do. And it's happening all over the state.
>
> "You know, the very fact that I'm talking to you like this, here today, puts me in jeopardy. Okay, and so, so be it. Okay, and I'm not *anti*, I'm not gay-bashing, but according

to God's word, that is not the right kind of lifestyle. It has deadly consequences for those people involved in it. They have more suicides and they're more discouraged, there's more illness, their life spans are shorter. You know, it's not a lifestyle that is good for this nation. Matter of fact, studies show no society that has totally embraced homosexuality has lasted more than, you know, a few decades. So it's the death knell for this country.

"I honestly think it's the biggest threat even, that our nation has, even more so than terrorism or Islam, which I think is a big threat, okay. Because what's happening now, they're going after, in schools, two year olds."

After watching the video a few times, I called the reporter back.

"You're right," I told him. "I do have plenty of comments."

He asked if he could film me that night at the conference. I said he could, and told him I'd make sure to alert the other ministers so they could be prepared as well.

As we were setting up for the conference, a campus security guard came to inform us that there was a small group of protesters outside. Paul Blair was leading the group, but there didn't appear to be any armed militia members. The guard assured us the protesters would be kept outside the building we were meeting in.

Trying to exhibit kindness, Mark suggested that the protesters at least be invited into the vestibule, as it was an unseasonably cold evening. The security guard disagreed.

"We think the best option is to keep them outside," he said. "You all have permission to be here; they do not."

We had a smaller-than-expected attendance, but some newly

out young people came, as did some parents whose children had just come out. We even welcomed a few pastors who were seeking help in ministering to the LGBT members of their congregations. Rep. Kern's speech was the talk of the crowd, and it attracted such a degree of media attention that our conference ended up as the opening story on that night's local news.

The local PFLAG chapter organized a rally at the state Capitol. Over three hundred people crowded into the basement of the rotunda. A handful of speeches were delivered denouncing the remarks and calling for an apology. Another minister, who was also a rhetoric professor, dissected Kern's speech with explanations of how her word choices constituted hate speech that contributed to an environment in which events like the Aryan Brotherhood murder could occur. The chair of the Cimarron Alliance Foundation called on the Speaker of the House to censure Kern. We closed the rally with everyone holding hands and singing "We Shall Overcome."

Rep. Kern and her allies held their own state Capitol rally two weeks later. More than one thousand people attended, many arriving on church buses. They sang hymns, prayed, and read scripture. Many ministers spoke.

Thanking her supporters, Kern said, "This is not about me. It's about the church having the right to speak out about the redeeming love of Jesus Christ who died to set us all free from our sins."

When the Cimarron Alliance Foundation learned Kern was scheduled to appear on *Flash Point*, the only show on TV that covered local politics, their leaders expressed concern over the possible public relations disaster that could result if the LGBT community was not also represented. Those leaders called on their connections, working to get someone from our community invited on the show. The producers eventually agreed. They would film the show on Good Friday, and the episode would air Easter Sunday morning. The producers left the decision on who would appear for the LGBT community up to the Cimarron Alliance Foundation. Rob Howard called to tell me who'd been chosen to represent us.

"Me?" I said, dumbfounded. "But it's a political debate show. Surely someone else is more qualified for that."

"The show's going to air on Easter morning. People will watch it before going to church. And we expect that her arguments will be mostly religious. We think you are the best spokesperson for countering her religious arguments."

He had made a good point, but I still had a reservation. "Yes, I could, but a television political debate show doesn't seem like the best forum for expounding different interpretations of the Bible."

He laughed, "Probably not. So don't do that. Stick to the simple message that many people read the Bible as welcoming to gay people. You are good at selecting a few key lines ahead of time and then sticking to them when you are being interviewed. That's made you an effective spokesperson."

"A skill I never expected to develop," I reminded him. "But thank you for saying that. However, a televised debate is very different from giving a statement that you know will be cut down to a few seconds."

"Yes, and you were a debater in high school. You speak in public every week. Don't sell yourself short."

"Okay." I was reluctantly beginning to agree.

Rob then added, "There's one more reason we think you would be good."

"What's that?" I wondered.

"Probably most Oklahomans have never seen a gay Christian, much less a gay minister. Just you being there will send an important message that she is wrong."

That reason persuaded me. "I'll do it, but you are coming with me for the filming."

"Done."

"You can even drive."

"No problem."

That week almost every gay leader in town called, emailed, or dropped by the house to give their advice and share information that I should use against Kern. But, there was too much information to include in the show, and also too much and sometimes conflicting advice. Rob and I settled on a couple key points.

First, Kern was notoriously aggressive. So we decided I should refrain from being aggressive in return. Instead, we hoped that my measured responses would draw out her aggression and exhibit a stark contrast.

Second, her main point had been a criticism of gay people in the political process. In her speech she had drawn particular attention to Jim Roth, who after his well-respected turn as an Oklahoma County Commissioner had been appointed by the governor to the Corporation Commission, the body that regulates utilities and the energy industry—a pretty powerful post in Oklahoma. Kern saw Jim's appointment as part of the gay takeover of America, threatening what she considered to be the country's identity as a Christian nation.

So I wanted to draw attention to the fact that she, an elected official, was basically saying that it was a threat for a segment of the population to be engaged in the political process by voting, lobbying, and organizing. Her argument appeared hypocritical to me.

On Good Friday afternoon, Rob and I drove to the television studio. We were greeted warmly in the lobby and escorted through the building, getting a mini-tour. Our enthusiastic guide showed us the new evening news set, in particular drawing our attention to the very large weather desk with its multiple screens while explaining the new technological capabilities of the set. Weather, of course, is the most important part of local TV in Oklahoma.

We ended the tour on the *Flashpoint* set, where we waited for the taping to begin. Kern arrived, escorted by a big man with a bushy black moustache. It was Paul Blair. I was taken aback to see him there. *Clearly all these anti-gay events are more coordinated than we realized*, I thought.

I introduced myself to Rep. Kern. The exchange wasn't warm, but it was polite, more so than I had anticipated.

Moments later, the hosts appeared and introduced themselves. We were invited to take our seats on the set. The techs attached our mics. Then, with almost no introduction, filming began.

Mike Turpen, the Democrat who appeared weekly on the show, started things off with a question for Kern.

"Do you think that Scott here is more dangerous than Osama bin Laden?"

Kern's response went on for about thirty seconds, but it never quite answered Turpen's question. She started by asserting that her criticisms were of something she called "the gay agenda" and not gay people individually. I stared directly at her the entire time while she sidestepped the question. After rambling on like this for a few more seconds, she finally looked at me.

"I don't know Scott personally, but he is individually not more dangerous than Osama bin Laden."

Well, I was glad that was established.

Kern did not refer to the Bible as often as we'd expected her to. But the Republican regular on the show did. Kirk Humphries was a real estate developer and former mayor who was then serving as chair of the Oklahoma City School Board. Despite the fact that he had no theological education, he kept trying to teach me what the Bible actually said. At one point, he asked me if I simply ignored the parts I didn't like.

I did my best to present a quick response about historical-critical reading of the Bible. I pointed out that there were many scholars, churches, and even entire denominations who disagreed with his reading of scripture. He kept coming back to adultery and wondering if I was excusing adultery. I refused to take the bait, calling that "a red herring." If you watch the video at this point you can see my lips are drawn tight and that I'm mustering all my strength to remain calm.

Eventually I declared that I felt attacked as a Christian, that Humphries and Kern were attacking my faith. At this point they quieted down and I was able to speak. I said that they were claiming I wasn't a Christian.

"Today I will enter my pulpit and preach about the resurrection of Jesus," I said to them. "About life and hope and compassion and liberation. Those are what the Gospel is about."

Kern then interrupted me for what someone later said was the forty-second time, and she gave her own statement about sin and said gay people were lost and needed salvation.

The filming ended and the guests were escorted out so that the regulars could film the closing and their commercial teasers for the week. In one of those teasers, real estate developer Humphries said that I had "bad theology."

When we got to the car, Rob turned to me and said, "You did a really good job. I don't know how you didn't reach across that desk and punch her and Humphries."

I told him that I had been suppressing my anger and offense for most of the taping.

"It's not every day that we have to sit politely at a table with people while they are insulting us to our faces," Rob said.

"Thank goodness," I responded. "I couldn't do that every day."

He started the car and as we drove out of the parking lot, he asked, "How do you feel?"

"Angry." Then I smiled, adding, "But I've been struggling to write my Easter sermon all week, occupied with this Kern nonsense. Now I know what I'm going to write."

Sitting down to write my sermon later that afternoon, I thought, *My faith has been challenged and insulted. This Easter sermon will tell the gospel as powerfully as I can tell it.*

On Sunday morning, Michael and I went to my parents' house for breakfast and to watch the show. I thought my mother was going to attack the television on more than one occasion.

"You did well," she said when the show ended. "I don't know how you controlled yourself. That is an evil woman. If I ever see her in public, I'll probably say that to her."

Michael admitted later that though he was sitting there watching with us, he hadn't really watched. He had purposely zoned out, knowing that he couldn't stand watching me be insulted and attacked.

I wasn't sure how I had done. I was second-guessing some of my measured responses. Maybe I had let her interrupt me too often. I wondered if I had served the LGBT community well.

On that Easter Sunday, our sanctuary was filled with lots of people who didn't normally attend. As I stepped forward to begin the welcome and announcements, the entire congregation rose in applause.

As I awkwardly smiled, waiting for the applause to die down, my self-doubt about my performance on the show melted away.

"Today I stand here proclaiming to you that God raised Jesus of Nazareth from the grave," I preached. I spoke of the new creation initiated by the resurrection and the political ramifications of those concepts.

> "In this Easter moment, God gave notice to the powers-that-be that their way is not God's way. That whenever they act against compassion, inclusion, and grace, they are acting against the power of God. That whenever they divide, exclude, or violently oppress, they are judged by the slaughtered and risen Lamb.
>
> "Yet, the powers-that-be continue to challenge the way of God in this world. They continue to sow darkness, doubt, and injury. They continue to preach that the way of God is division, exclusion, and violent oppression of those different from themselves. The Risen One stands to rebuke

them. This is not the way of God. It is the way of Caesar. It is the way of sin. It is the path to hell.

"We will not be thwarted by their failed philosophies and false doctrines, because we share in the power of the Risen One. We too have been raised with Christ."

And then I closed,

"It is with passionate faith that today I stand here and proclaim to you that when God raised Jesus of Nazareth from the grave, God raised you up to a new life. With courage and hope let us go forth and bear witness that we are alive!"

The congregation applauded again, rising to their feet. Later, Paula Sophia sent me an email:

> "At this point in my life, it's easy for me to feel beat down and overcome with cynicism, to retreat from Christianity, and it would have been a horrible thing for me to contemplate having to preach an Easter sermon right on the heels of experiencing such an outrageous injustice.
>
> "You preached with such conviction, such power! From where I sat, I did not see a hurt and resentful young man; I saw a battle-tested soul who will not let go of faith, and I felt convicted in my own absence from the dialogue of faith lately.
>
> "In one day, to see you beat down and then to watch you rise up in that pulpit. Wow! That's Easter!"

After church that night, Michael and I stopped at Walgreen's to pick up a few household supplies. As we exited the store and headed to our car, a panhandler came up to us. He appeared about to ask us for money, when he paused and looked closely at me.

"Hey," he said. "You were on TV this morning weren't you?"

A little surprised, I said, "Yes, I was."

"Good job. Keep up the good work."

Thoroughly astonished and also excited, I thanked him.

He walked away from us without asking for any money. Then he stopped a lady getting out her car, but instead of asking her for money, he pointed to me.

"Did you see this guy on TV this morning?" he said. "He was on with that anti-gay state representative, Sally Kern. He's a gay man, a minister even, and he was defending his rights."

The very startled-looking woman said, "I don't agree with that. I think being gay is a sin." She began to rush into the store.

"What?" the man called after her. "Really? You should talk to him and let him convince you otherwise." He turned back to me. "Go talk to her," he said.

"Thanks, but she seemed a little afraid."

He smiled at me. "Well, have a good evening and keep up the good work."

25

Tangelo

Saturday, February 7, 2009 was unusually warm, and everyone wanted to be outside.

"I'm going for a walk!" I said to Michael. "Come with me."

"I think I'm going to the gym. I haven't been all week."

"Okay, but why work out inside when the day is so lovely?" I implored.

"Enjoy your walk," he said. "See you later."

"Your loss."

I grabbed an issue of *The New Yorker* and headed out, planning to walk two or three times around Edgemere Park while reading. John Updike had just died, and the magazine had published pages of excerpts from his stories that had run in the magazine over the years.

On my second lap around the park, I was reading an Updike story in which a young man was driving and at the end of his journey there was a girl who wanted to marry him.

I thought, *At the end of my journey is a guy who wants to marry me.*

Michael had told me not long before that he wanted to marry me. He said he knew I hadn't yet decided whether

I wanted that or not, but that he wanted me to know that when I decided, he'd be ready.

I thought again, with mounting astonishment, *There's a guy who wants to marry me? Why don't I want to marry him?*

I realized I *did* want to marry him.

At this point I was at the far corner of the park where a grove of tall trees encloses a space near the creek. I had often wandered through that grove when I was contemplating a sermon.

"Okay," an internal voice said. "Then you need to ask him to marry you."

Another internal voice responded, "Don't you need to think about it some more?"

"No, I don't need to think about it. He wants to marry me, and I want to marry him. We are getting married."

How should I ask him? I thought. It would take some time to plan.

From the cacophony in my head, I heard, "You don't need to plan anything. Ask him today."

"But it won't be romantic."

"Sure it will. Just asking will be romantic."

"Okay, then. I will."

I confidently returned to reading Updike stories as I walked home. When I arrived, Michael was still at the gym, so I went inside and grabbed a glass of ice water and a tangelo, then went to sit on one of the old red metal chairs on the back patio. I drank the water and peeled the tangelo as I finished the Updike excerpts. Soon Michael pulled up in his new Corolla.

He got out wearing a sweaty t-shirt and gym shorts. I was also wearing a sweaty t-shirt and gym shorts. As he got his gym bag out of the back, he glanced over at me with a puzzled look on his face. It was as if he'd spotted a change in me and was trying to figure out what it was. But he didn't say anything. Instead, he walked over and sat down on the other chair.

"Want a piece of tangelo?" I asked.

"Sure," he said. And as he reached for the piece I was handing him, I said, "Marry me."

He looked directly at me, pausing for a few seconds before asking, "Is that a proposal?"

"Yes. Marry me."

His eyes opened wider, his face brightened, and he exclaimed, "Yes, yes. A thousand times yes."

Al McAffrey, my state representative, had invited me to be Chaplain of the Day for the Oklahoma House of Representatives. The various members take turns inviting faith leaders to perform the mostly ceremonial role. The chaplain is given a reserved parking space and can enter the Capitol through one of the doors not open to the general public.

Al had been elected to the legislature my first year back in Oklahoma City. He was in his fifties, often wore cowboy boots, and came across as something of a good ol' boy. That persona served him well as the first openly gay member of the Oklahoma legislature. He owned a big home in one of the historic sections of Oklahoma City, where he hosted parties that mixed the LGBT community with state leaders. He and I had actually gone on a date back when I was single.

When I got to Al's office, he said, "Everyone's waiting to see what Sally Kern does."

I laughed. "I'm sure."

"It'll be fine. This is all rather routine. In a moment we'll go down, and the ushers will walk you through the protocol." He asked if I had guests with me.

I answered that Michael, my parents, and some church members and friends were planning to be there for the opening prayer.

"You do know that you can introduce them first, but that you must ask the permission of the Speaker?"

I told him the printed instructions I'd received ahead of time had explained the procedure.

Shortly we headed down to the chamber. Al introduced me to the usher, who walked me through the protocol—what chair I was supposed to sit in as the session began, when I would be invited up to the dais, how I was supposed to walk up there.

"When you walk up, the Speaker will reach out a hand for you to shake," he said. "If you have any guests to introduce— do you have guests to introduce?"

I told him I did.

"Most people do. You then thank the Speaker for the opportunity to pray and ask for permission to introduce your guests in the gallery. He will grant it, and then you can turn, greet your guests, and deliver the prayer."

I responded that it all seemed straightforward. He then told me to enjoy myself.

Al wandered back over. "When you are done with the prayer, we'll go to the members' lobby in back and take a photo. You should tell Michael and your parents to join us for that. Then, if you want, you can come sit at my desk with me. You are welcome to stay all day if you'd like."

I told him I'd probably take him up on the offer. As something of a politics geek, I knew I'd enjoy watching the session from the floor.

The chair I was supposed to wait in was close to one of the two back entrances to the legislative chamber. It was an entrance used only by members and their staff. As the chamber began to fill up, some people who knew me stopped to say hello, including Kris Steele. Kris was a GOP representative from Shawnee who had been our freshman class president at OBU. I had voted for him when he first ran, and he's also godfather to my nephews.

Minutes before the session was to open, Rep. Sally Kern entered through the door nearest me and walked directly over. I stood as she reached out her hand, "Reverend Jones, it is good to see you again. Welcome to the House."

"Thank you," I answered. "It's good to be here."

"We will look forward to your prayer." She grinned.

"Thank you," I said and she turned away.

As I sat back down, I noticed that many of the members had been watching the exchange.

Then, the session began. The Speaker called the room to order and soon I was invited forward. I walked up to the dais. As instructed, I shook hands with the Speaker and asked for permission to introduce my guests in the gallery. He gave me permission.

I then turned to the rostrum and began.

"Today I thank you for the opportunity to be present with

you as chaplain for the day. I want to thank my representative and good friend, the Honorable Al McAffrey, for the invitation. I would also like to acknowledge guests who are present in the gallery – members of my congregation, the Cathedral of Hope, United Church of Christ. Joining them are dear friends, my wonderful parents, and my loving partner Michael Cich."

On the hard copy of my manuscript I had called Michael my fiancé, but I decided at the last minute not to say that word, even though it was true. I didn't say fiancé for two reasons. We hadn't yet told all our friends and family that we were engaged; it had only been a few days since I'd proposed. Also, the word fiancé seemed sure to be inflammatory. I was the first out gay minister to serve as chaplain anyway, probably the first person to introduce my same-sex partner as a guest in the gallery, so I saw no need to push the bounds any further.

After my introduction, I prayed. At the close of the prayer, Al and I went to the lobby and waited for my parents and Michael in order to take the picture. Then they departed to return to work, and I went to sit with Al. I enjoyed watching the legislative process. Many of the representatives stopped by to say hello and to commend the prayer. One reminded Al that later he needed to make the routine motion of having the prayer entered into the record. I was told I'd need to submit a copy. One of the ushers asked, "Can we have your hard copy?"

"Sure, there are a few edits and handwritten notes on it. I'll send a clean copy by email if you want."

"Do both," he instructed.

At the end of the session, when all the significant business was complete, Kris Steele was now sitting in the Speaker's chair and the duty fell to him to run through the routine unanimous consent motions. Al rose to make the motion that the chaplain of the day's prayer be entered into the record.

And then someone on the other side of the room objected.

Suddenly, representatives who had been barely paying attention began to look around and ask what was going on. Several of them started asking questions of the chair. Kris looked confused. I later learned that this was the first time in state history that someone had objected to entering the prayer into the record, thus requiring the chamber to vote on a prayer.

Kris regained control of the room and called for a vote on whether to enter the chaplain's prayer into the record. One of Al's colleagues noted that a number of members seemed to be scurrying for the doors. He grabbed his microphone and announced to the room, "I want to remind all members of the House that if they can hear my voice, they need to vote." The final vote showed that fifteen members who had been there moments before had escaped.

Twenty voted against entering my prayer into the record. Kern was one of them, though she wasn't the one who originally objected. The overwhelming majority, even of Republicans, voted for putting the prayer into the record.

I sat there the entire time feeling amused. Al and his colleagues were apologetic. As the session came to an end, even Rep. Steele offered his apologies.

On the way home, I called Michael to tell him about it. He got upset. But I thought the entire episode was funny.

The next morning when I was eating breakfast and Michael was still asleep in bed, I got a text message from a friend.

Great article on the cover of today's Oklahoman.

I replied, *What?*

Front-page story about your prayer yesterday and the vote.

I guess I need to look at the paper.

I looked online, and there was the announcement that a gay minister's prayer had been objected to because he introduced his fiancé. They even had a link to a PDF of the hard copy of my prayer, with my handwritten marks and edits.

I walked into the bedroom and woke Michael up. "Guess what? We are the first gay couple to have our engagement announced on the front page of *The Daily Oklahoman.*"

Still half-sleepy, Michael asked, "What?"

I repeated the news and showed him the article.

"But I haven't told all my family yet," he complained.

"Well, they are going to know now."

The President and General Minister of the United Church of Christ issued a public statement objecting to the legislature voting on prayers. The heads of other denominations did as well. Separation of church and state organizations wrote that here was good evidence for why there should be no prayers in public bodies. My fellow progressive clergy called a press conference in the Capitol rotunda to denounce the votes against the prayer. Columnists opined on the issue, including some who said I shouldn't have said anything so inflammatory as fiancé. Only the article in the *Edmond Sun* noted that I didn't say fiancé; evidently they had listened to the audio recording which was publicly available.

Every day that week, *The Oklahoman* ran a story about my prayer and the fallout. Each time they called on readers to write to the twenty legislators and tell them what they thought about voting on prayers.

The next week, Westboro Baptist Church from Topeka, Kansas—those infamous "God hates fags" protesters—came to demonstrate outside the "pro-gay" Oklahoma House of Representatives. Pro-gay because the majority hadn't voted against my prayer, and because I'd even been allowed to pray in the first place.

That week I received a call from a friend of mine, a military veteran living in Alabama.

"Have you read the comments on the news stories?" he asked.

I laughed. "No, I never read the comments."

"Then don't," he responded, not laughing. "But listen to me when I tell you not to sit with your back to the window, either."

I wasn't sure if he was overreacting, but I took his advice for the weeks following the story.

I declined to answer when a reporter from *The Daily Oklahoman* asked when and where I was getting married. Michael and I later turned down a request from the *Oklahoma Gazette*, for whom I was then a columnist, to cover our wedding. They wanted to put a photo of the wedding on the front cover. Instead, I wrote my monthly column about the meaning of our marriage. They invited Rep. Kern to write a rebuttal, which she did.

Mom said she thought we should hire security for the wedding.

I told her we already had.

26

We have already won.

"We can just have simple finger foods instead of a meal."

Michael looked at me like I was stupid. "You do realize I'm Filipino?" he said. "Do you know nothing about my culture?"

"I'm not sure what you mean." Clearly, I knew very little about his culture.

He took his time to respond. "My mother is not going to be satisfied with finger foods. There will be a full meal. There will even be enough food for everyone to take some home with them. That's traditional."

"Okay," I said, wondering how complicated this was going to be.

"I'm just telling you," he said emphatically.

The ceremony was four months off. We had decided to hold it in the grove of trees by the creek in Edgemere Park. The reception would be at our house. We expected two hundred guests. We thought these arrangements would be simpler to plan and less expensive than a more formal alternative. I've since learned there is no such thing as a simple wedding, especially with two hundred guests. And while our plans cost us less than some options might have, the wedding wasn't inexpensive.

We began compiling the long wedding preparations to-do list.

Our parents came over for dinner the next week in order to discuss plans. With a same-sex couple, of course, the roles and obligations of each family are not obvious. As Michael had predicted, his mom immediately said she'd be responsible for the wedding reception.

"We must have roast pork, of course. That's traditional," she said.

Normally she'd roast the pig herself in the backyard, Michael explained to me later. But this time she decided to order the pig roasted by the Asian grocery store.

"You do realize that it will be an entire pig?" he asked me.

I had not.

We decided to create a menu using both families' cultural traditions as a theme. We'd serve lumpia from the Philippines and sauerkraut and brats to reflect Michael's German side.

"What are your cultural foods?" Michael asked.

Mom answered for me. "We can just go Oklahoman. How about barbecue brisket?"

"Yeah," I said. "That sounds good. I'm guessing chicken fried steak is out of the question?"

Mom replied, "How about fried chicken for the rehearsal dinner?"

Michael smiled at this. "You know fried chicken is my favorite food?"

"Yes," Mom said. "So fried chicken will work for everyone. I'll take care of that dinner."

We left with all the roles decided.

Next we met with Paula Sophia's wife, who was a florist. We wanted her insight on what vendors we could use—those who wouldn't reject the business of a gay couple. She gave us a list. In fact, there were so many vendors open to working with a gay couple, we were able to shop around. In 2009 in Oklahoma City, we got no grief. No vendor we approached had any problems working with us. Everyone was welcoming and helpful.

Once the weather was consistently warm, we started working on the backyard. Michael had always hated the overgrown patch in the back. He was determined to remove all the undergrowth, trim the lower branches, and sow grass seeds so we could put tables under the trees. I thought he was being overly ambitious. He was, but we got the work done. Fortunately we had lots of pleasant weather that spring and enough rain that the new lawn came in beautifully.

"We can't get married with you never having met my grandparents and the rest of the Minnesota Ciches," Michael said to me one day. "We have to plan a trip to Minneapolis."

"Okay," I said sarcastically. "We'll fit that into our four months of preparations."

The day we left for Minneapolis, we had to delay getting on the road because our invitations were just being finished by the printer, more than a week late. As we drove north we took turns driving and stuffing envelopes. Batches got mailed from various post offices throughout the Midwest.

Just a month before, in the midst of our wedding preparations, the Iowa Supreme Court had ruled that that state's ban on same-sex marriage was unconstitutional. The Sunday following that ruling, I walked to the front of the chancel at church during the announcement time and said,

"We have already won. The ruling in Iowa this week confirms it. Iowa. Just think of it. The center of the American heartland. If we can win same-sex marriage rights in Iowa, we have won the first and most important contest—the struggle for hearts and minds. It may take twenty years for us to mop up our victory—for all the courts to rule and the laws to be passed—but we now know victory is inevitable. We have won."

The congregation applauded. Some of them cried.

Since our route to Minneapolis took us through Des Moines, Michael and I decided to visit the Iowa State Capitol. We noticed that a number of downtown Des Moines businesses were flying rainbow flags. Inside the Capitol, we found the Supreme Court chamber and sat momentarily, paying our respects.

Back on the road, an hour outside Minneapolis, Michael was behind the wheel.

"There's something I need to tell you." he said.

I was still stuffing wedding invitations. "Okay," I said. "What?"

"My dad called the other day. He said he needed to tell me something."

When Michael did not continue, I asked, "What did he tell you?"

"He said that he hadn't yet told the Minneapolis family that we are getting married."

That surprised me. I had somehow thought that they were throwing us a shower while we were there. Michael explained that there was a family party planned for Saturday at his aunt and uncle's, but that it wouldn't be a shower.

"No problem," I shrugged. "We'll just announce the wedding

to the rest of the family and hand out the invitations at the party." I went back to stuffing.

A minute later, Michael turned his head slightly toward me and said, "There's something else."

Now my attention was riveted on him.

He took a deep breath. "Dad also said he's never told any of the Minnesota family that I'm gay."

This news was a completely different matter than their not knowing that we were getting married in five weeks. In less than an hour, Michael and I were meeting up with most of his father's family for dinner at a pizza place. Suddenly the trip took on a very different tone.

"Surely," I said, working to process this new information, "if they know you are bringing a guy to meet them, then they know you're gay."

There was hesitation in his voice. "You would assume that," he said.

Suddenly thinking about the coming night, I asked, "The aunt and uncle we are staying with know, right?" I was imagining an awkward moment when the time came to go to bed.

Michael assured me that they did. So after mulling over this news, I told him I wasn't going to be worried. If some of the family knew, then surely everything would be okay.

After thinking a moment longer, I asked, "Why are you just now telling me? We've been driving for twelve hours stretched over two days."

"There was no reason for you to worry the entire drive." He flashed a mischievous smile. "Now you've only got a few minutes to worry."

"Great," I said sarcastically. "Thank you for that."

So we arrived at the pizza place and I was introduced to various cousins, aunts, uncles, and to Grandpa Ted. No one seemed to blink. They were, in fact, all incredibly welcoming, asking me lots of questions.

Michael's Aunt Jackie said, "Scott, tell us all about everything going on with the family in Oklahoma. Michael's dad never tells us anything."

I laughed heartily. I had begun to pick up that they knew more about me than Michael's announcement on the road had suggested. Finally I ventured to tell Aunt Jackie that Michael's dad had said no one in Minnesota knew that Michael and I were dating.

"Yet it seems like you all knew already," I said. "What's the explanation?"

"Simple," she answered. "I read your blog."

"Oh?" I was shocked at this revelation, but I was also relieved that the weekend wasn't going to be awkward. And I was glad I had chosen not to worry that last hour following Michael's bombshell.

The entire table was now paying attention to my conversation with Jackie. Relieved that they all knew Michael was gay and that we were dating, I was now curious to find out how this aunt in Minnesota had discovered my blog.

Jackie explained that Michael's dad was really bad at sharing news, as I had already learned.

"We have to find out about the Oklahoma Ciches other ways," she said. "For years I've Googled family members to see what I could find out about them. A few years ago, it must have been shortly after you started dating, I Googled Michael and found where you had written about him on your blog. So I've been following your relationship all along and passing along news to the rest of the family."

Michael and I laughed. I could tell he was as relieved as I was.

"So, you knew Michael was gay?" I asked. "Michael's dad feared that none of you up here knew."

Aunt Mona Rae said, "I think we've all suspected Michael was gay since he was a little kid."

Everyone laughed again.

The next day Michael and I met up with Grandpa Ted in order to go visit his Grandma Marion in the nursing home where she lived. Marion had dementia. Some days were better than others, Ted told us. Most of the time she knew her close family. Ted visited her twice every day, still taking his meals with her.

When we arrived for our visit, she was in the community room. I saw her brighten when she saw Ted. When she saw Michael behind him, her face brightened even more.

"Michael!" she called out.

"Grandma!" he said as he rushed over and hugged her.

Then she looked up at me. "This must be Scott."

That story has become a family legend. How did she know my name? Because all those years Aunt Jackie had been printing photos of Michael and me that she found on my blog and hanging them on Marion's wall among all the other family photos.

On Saturday we went to the family party at Ken and Mona Rae's house. All the nearby family came, even Aunt Mary, who drove down from Ely in the Boundary Waters. Cousin Tina lived in Arizona, but she also happened to be home that weekend. The house was full of Ciches.

After everyone had arrived, Michael got their attention. "Everyone, I have an announcement to make," he said.

"Oh, this is going to be good," Aunt Mary said, grabbing a seat in front of Michael.

"The reason Scott and I came to visit is so I could introduce him to all of you, because we are getting married on June 6, and you are all invited."

Cheers and applause went up around the room. I started passing around the invitations.

"What's that?" Grandma Marion asked. She was seated in the back of the room in her wheelchair and had difficulty hearing.

Uncle Ken said, "Michael and Scott are getting married. Here's the invitation."

Marion looked at it. "Getting married? Oh? Isn't that strange." Cousins giggled.

Ken then sat down with his parents and explained everything to them. At the end of the conversation Marion said, "I'm going to go."

Ted said, "We'll have to see about that."

Marion didn't get to make the trip in June, and she was really angry about it. Ted told all his kids that he expected them to be at the wedding. Even conservative Uncle Dave who lived in Texas came. Our wedding was the first time all of Michael's dad's siblings had been together in almost twenty years.

Pappoo didn't attend the wedding. My Aunt Karen came, but neither of my uncles did. Harley prepared barbecue for us, but he had another obligation that weekend. Unlike every other wedding in our family where everyone swarmed in, I had this tiny contingent, and Michael had a horde from all over the country. Mom was embarrassed and hurt. As was I. It was a hurt that hasn't gone away.

A church member named Edward had offered his bright red convertible T-bird for our use at the wedding. We told no one else, not even our family or wedding party. We sent them all over to the park before Edward arrived at our house. He had installed the parade bench he used every year for the gay pride parade. We sat on the bench like grand marshals or beauty queens.

The drive to the park was a couple blocks. When we were close enough to see the crowd seated under the trees beside the creek, you could hear the reaction as they noticed and began to point, cheer, and applaud. We scored on the grand entrance.

Michael and I walked down hand in hand from the streetside to the area behind all the white chairs full of guests. We met our family and the wedding party and went over last-minute instructions for how to go down the aisle. Then the string quartet struck up Bach's "Air on the G String," and the processional began.

We had two aisles, so Michael's family and attendants went down one side and mine down the other. We each had five people standing with us. His brother Robert and four close friends. I had my sister Erin (who had just given birth to my second nephew), Rob, Tim, Jason from high school, and Marty, one of my close friends from college. Jason was the best man. Harry Wooten, from Royal Lane, was the officiant.

OPEN

Michael and I walked down the two aisles. We met again in front. I had just turned to face him when I noticed a person crouching behind a bush across the creek. The person was holding something and pointing it in our direction.

Well, I guess this is it, I thought. *This is when I die.*

Then I noticed that our security guard was approaching the person. After a few seconds, when no rifle shot had felled me, I turned my attention back to my wedding.

Later I learned she was a neighbor taking photos with a camera. She hid behind the bush because she didn't want to be visible. That was a big fail, as she alarmed a number of guests who saw her hiding.

In front of two hundred guests representing every facet of our lives—childhood, high school, college, and every job and church we had been a part of, plus a huge contingent from the Oklahoma City gay and activist communities—we said our vows.

Michael's mother had ordered two entire roast pigs for the reception. One was butchered and set up in chafing dishes. The other one was lying in its entirety in the middle of our buffet table, with a sunflower in its mouth. Our vegetarian friends were horrified.

Before everyone left, my mother-in-law had the pig moved to the breakfast table and began to butcher it, placing the meat in Ziploc bags so that the guests could take the tasty pork home with them.

Watching how my mother-in-law handled a knife as she expertly carved up that hog, I knew I'd never hurt her son.

"Did you see the state Republican party platform?" Michael asked me. He had just come home from work, and I was sitting at my desk.

"Yes. And all its anti-gay stuff," I answered.

He shook his head. "But did you also see where the platform mentioned you and me?" he asked.

"What? No!" I exclaimed, turning around in my seat. "Where was that?"

"Page twenty-nine.," he said, walking over to my desk. "They don't mention us by name, but it's obviously us."

So, I pulled the new state Republican Party platform back up on my computer, scrolled down to page 29, and there at the top of the page was this:

We commend state Representatives Wright, Blackwell, Christian, Coody, Duncan, Enns, Faught, Johnson, Kern, Key, Liebmann, Moore, Murphey, Osborn, Ownbey, Reynolds, Ritze, Sanders, Terrill, and Thomsen for opposing inclusion in the House Journal, the introduction of an openly homosexual minister's male "fiancé".

Now the state party was on record commending the twenty representatives who had opposed the prayer. Rob Howard noticed the paragraph as well and wrote a letter to the editor of the *Daily Oklahoman*, which they didn't publish, but which I thought was hilarious. It said, in part, "Glad to see that the Oklahoma GOP recognizes in their state party platform that gay men can be ministers and have fiancés."

27

Tootsie Roll Pop

Mom was all dressed up and smiling. She was riding with us to the Oklahoma History Center, the state museum located in a fun modern building across from the State Capitol. And by fun, I mean the building looks from the outside like an old oil can stuck in the middle of a cement block. The museum was the location for the first annual LGBT History Month Dinner hosted by the Cimarron Alliance Foundation. Mom was coming with us because I was receiving the Torch Award.

The Torch Award is one of a series of awards Cimarron gives recognizing contributions to and on behalf of the LGBT community of Oklahoma. They give awards to young leaders, journalists, legislators, and others who have made significant contributions toward equality. The Torch Award is "reserved for a person who is an exemplary representative of the LGBT community; one who allows the light of equality to shine in her or his words, actions, and interactions with others."

After dinner, when I was called to the front to receive my award and give brief remarks, I shared the story of that day in 1994 when I was a sophomore at Oklahoma Baptist University and Matt Cox told me the news about the university's disciplining of Sean Baugh.

"I paced my dorm room that afternoon, deciding what I was going to do," I stated. "Would I be a person of integrity and step forward to challenge the school's anti-gay policy, maybe bringing down retribution on myself or inciting suspicion as to my own sexuality? Or would I take the easier route and say and do nothing?"

I looked around a room full of far more seasoned activists than me. "I chose to be a person of integrity," I continued. "It was the first time I stood up for gay rights. In some way, everything I've done since has been because of the decision I made that day. So if I have contributed anything to the cause of LGBT rights here in Oklahoma, it is because I knew that what was done to Sean was wrong, and I never wanted anything like that to happen again."

As 2009 rolled into 2010, my public influence in Oklahoma City was rising. I had a popular monthly column in the *Oklahoma Gazette.* I was serving on nonprofit boards of directors. The Philosophy Department at the University of Oklahoma invited me to be their alumni speaker that year. I regularly received invitations to speak at churches, colleges, and nonprofits. And I was invited to join a small group of progressive leaders who met over Chinese food to strategize how to make Oklahoma better.

Pappoo even seemed to be coming around.

Sue, my step-grandmother, died that fall. Michael came with me to the funeral and visited Pappoo's house for the first time. Everyone was very polite.

Shortly before the holidays, we received a note from Pappoo inviting the two of us to come to Christmas. For three years we had been absent, as had Mom.

Michael was nervous when we arrived for the holiday, but no drama ensued. Pappoo didn't even try to hand him a religious tract.

When it came time for Pappoo to pass out his Christmas gifts to the family, he walked over to where Michael sat.

"Michael, here's your gift," he said. Pappoo then handed Michael a Tootsie Roll Pop with a $20 bill wrapped around the stem. It was the same gift he was giving to all the grandkids and their spouses.

"Thank you," Michael said. He looked at me and grinned. I saw Mom dab a tear from the corner of her eye.

Despite all these improvements in our shared life, I was looking for a job, applying to churches around the country. When I began the process, I asked Michael if there were any limitations on where I could search. "Not Arizona," he answered. "I don't like Arizona. It's too dry."

Cathedral of Hope Oklahoma City had been a five-year-old congregation when I arrived, having been served by three pastors in those five years. I was coming up on my fifth year there. We had not continued to grow, as we had hoped. We had for the first two years, but then we plateaued and attendance and participation began to drop off. Once we became an independent congregation in 2007, without the financial and administrative largesse of the mother church in Dallas, we had

struggled as well. I had difficulty recruiting and training volunteers to fill all the roles that for many years had been covered
by the large staff in Dallas. The Great Recession didn't help,
either. It hit just as we became independent. We had depleted
the $12,000 reserve Cathedral of Hope Dallas had given us
when we separated. One time I had to take a member to lunch
and implore him to donate enough money to cover my salary
for that month.

Our congregation had affiliated with the United Church
of Christ in 2006. The UCC was the most liberal and socially
active of the mainline Protestant denominations. It had been
formed in 1957 when the Congregational Christian Churches
and the Evangelical and Reformed Church merged, uniting
the old New England WASP establishment with a primarily German immigrant, Midwestern church. The UCC had
since acquired liberal churches from a variety of traditions.
The denomination's largest churches are now predominately
African-American, like Trinity in Chicago, whose former
pastor Jeremiah Wright became a big news story during the
Obama campaign in 2008.

The UCC is also famous for its firsts. It was the first
denomination to ordain an African-American, and the first
to ordain a woman. It was also the first Mainline Protestant
church to ordain an openly gay man. Its national meeting,
the General Synod, embraced marriage equality for same-sex
couples in 2005.

Our congregation held a series of educational forums to
learn about the UCC. During one of these, church member
Peter Keltch asked, "But aren't these the people who burned

witches in Salem? I'm not sure I want to be associated with witch burners."

The person leading the forum said, "That was centuries ago. They've come a long way since then."

Peter responded, "Still. I'm not sure I want to associate with that history."

The vote was unanimous in our congregation.

Centuries before, some of my ancestors were among those who departed the Massachusetts Bay Colony in order to go with Roger Williams to found Providence and the first Baptist church in America. At that time, those Baptist ancestors were the more progressive, having left the more traditional Puritan church. Now I had made the reverse move, but for the same reasons.

Despite our congregation's financial and administrative struggles, we had continued to perform ministry that helped people and changed lives. Young adults contacted us for help coming out to families. Middle-aged folks would come to us for help as they came out, too, often after a divorce. We continued our service projects in the community, even growing a Health Ministry that provided free annual flu shots on the Gay Strip. One year we gave them on Halloween night. I'll never forget the young man who came in to get a shot on that chilly autumn night wearing only skimpy Superman underwear and calling it his costume.

In the fall of 2009, I told the church I was looking for a job and organized an aggressive, short-term effort to get the church in a better position financially. We formed a series of task forces who focused on various aspects of congregational life. These groups did great work.

One group looked at our building situation. Since the church's founding, they had rented space at the First Unitarian Church for worship on Sunday evenings. Though many people wanted us to find our own building, the finances were simply not available. Rev. Robin Meyers, Senior Minister of Mayflower Congregational Church, learned that we were looking and offered us use of their sanctuary and fellowship hall on a Sunday evening for free (though an occasional donation to the church would be welcome).

On a cold, wintry evening, we gathered to contemplate the offer and take a vote on whether to move from the only space the church had known for ten years. After an emotional discussion, the vote was taken and the proposal to move was approved. We then began planning a leave-taking service. On our final Sunday at First Unitarian church, members carried out the various elements of our worship—communion chalice and paten, altar candles, paraments, etc. I exited last, bearing the cross.

The next Sunday, many people joined us as guests to celebrate moving into the new space. We gathered in the fellowship hall with all the elements we had carried out the week before, this time carrying them into the sanctuary that would be our new home.

Attendance began to improve, as did finances. We offered some new classes and programs and became more aggressive in our use of social media. Most everyone worked very hard over those six months, always with the uncertainty about when I might depart.

When the April financial report came out, I was able to announce to the congregation that for the first time in its ten-year history, the church was in the black. The good news was a sign that the hard work of the last six months had borne fruit.

The next week I announced that I was leaving for Omaha, Nebraska.

That winter I had noticed First Central Congregational Church in Omaha on the United Church of Christ job listings. I was sitting in my home office while Michael was watching TV in the living room. After pondering for a few minutes, I called out, "What do you think of Omaha?"

Michael, who knew I was looking at job listings, hesitated for a few moments before answering.

"I don't think anything about Omaha," he said.

"Do you mind if I apply to a church there?"

"No, I don't," he answered.

So I did. And soon I heard back from the church's search committee that I had made the first cut, and they wanted to talk further. After a phone interview, they flew me and Michael up for a weekend in March.

I had never been to Nebraska. Michael had visited a couple of times when friends of his had been students at the University of Nebraska in Lincoln, but he had never been to Omaha. When we departed the plane at Eppley Airfield, we didn't expect the forested hills we saw through the window. "That's Nebraska?" Michael asked.

"I guess so," I answered. "Not what I expected."

Later we learned that those forested hills were actually Iowa.

We were to meet a woman named Jan who was moderator of the church, the elected lay leader who ran the church council. Though she had seen pictures of us, we didn't know what she looked like. But as we exited the gates, I said to Michael, "That gray-haired woman with glasses standing over there looks like a UCC person. I bet that's Jan."

"You're right," he said with a laugh.

Soon we were getting a tour of Omaha, including where Warren Buffett's house is. Then we saw the church. For five years I had now pastored a small, mostly LGBT congregation only ten years old and without a building or staff. First Central was over 150 years old and was located in a large, beautiful downtown building from the 1920s. The church employed five staff members, including a part-time minister who assisted with visitation. The congregation was almost four hundred people, 98 percent of whom were straight.

First Central is one of the oldest Protestant churches in town. Her founders were among the founders of the city and the state. The congregation had enjoyed a history of prominence in the city. Like most downtown churches, First Central had experienced a decline in membership since the 1960s, when people began moving to the suburbs.

A church volunteer named Tom showed Michael and I around the building. He was in his late seventies and had been a pillar of the church for forty years, volunteering almost daily since he retired, helping with building maintenance and anything else that needed to be done. Touring the building with Tom, all Michael and I saw was opportunity. For five years I had been in a situation where I had desired more space for ministry, and here was abundant space. More, even, than the congregation knew what to do with.

Plus, the neighborhood was about to change. A major new

development called Midtown Crossing was being constructed just a few blocks away. Filled with high-rise condos and apartments, the development also included a cinema, hotel, and many bars, restaurants, and shops. Mutual of Omaha was funding the project. I enjoyed seeing the Mutual corporate headquarters bearing the famous Native American chief's head logo, which I fondly recalled from watching *Mutual of Omaha's Wild Kingdom* every Sunday as a child.

And of course we liked the people we met. This visit was limited to the search committee, their spouses, and the church staff. They took us to Sunday brunch in a gay-owned restaurant called *Dixie Quicks* that was filled with radical, erotic art and served Southern cuisine.

Michael and I flew home to Oklahoma City after the weekend and had to wait weeks while First Central completed interviews with the other finalists. In early April, they called and offered me the job. I accepted. We had, of course, hoped to move to a state where there were more laws protecting gay people and our relationships, but this particular congregation was such a great fit with my own talents and values that we felt this was where we were being called.

In early May we returned to Omaha for my "candidating weekend." In the United Church of Christ, the candidate for pastor visits the church, getting to know the members, who hear the candidate preach and then vote on whether to extend the call. Before that weekend, I asked Jan what percentage of the vote would be too low for me accept the call.

"What do you mean?" she asked.

"Most pastors won't accept a job if 10% of the congregation

votes no," I told her. "Even if the bylaws state the vote only has to be two-thirds or three-fourths, most ministers wouldn't want to deal with an opposition the size of ten percent."

Then I explained to her that when a church is breaking a barrier, like calling its first female pastor or its first openly gay pastor, there can sometimes be a significant percentage of opposition. In those circumstances, the general rule of thumb is sometimes suspended and the minister will go ahead and accept the job.

"So," I asked her again. "How much opposition is too much?"

She looked puzzled. "I don't know. I'll ask others, but Scott, what you are talking about is not going to be a problem. There will not be a sizable opposition. If there is, then we haven't done our jobs well as a search committee, understanding the congregation and what they are looking for in a new pastor. And I'm confident we have done our job well. This will not be an issue, I assure you."

On Saturday night the church held a potluck dinner so people from the congregation could meet me and Michael. I was to give an opening speech, and then there would be a question-and-answer session. The congregants arriving for dinner were enthusiastic in welcoming us. I was introduced as everyone was finishing dinner.

"I want to begin by addressing something that I know is a concern for some of you," I said. The room became deathly silent. "Yes, I am a Sooner fan." There was loud laughter and a big release of tension.

I was told only three people voted against extending the call.

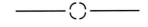

Back in Oklahoma City, my physician offered me anxiety pills before I informed the Cathedral of Hope congregation that I was leaving.

My final Sunday, almost two hundred people attended the worship service and reception. The congregation was filled with church members we hadn't seen in a while, clergy colleagues, politicians, our families, and lots of activist friends. There were even quite a few atheists. In the liturgical calendar, that day was Trinity Sunday, so when I got up to speak I said it had all been a ruse to get all these Unitarians and atheists to church so they could hear a sermon on the Trinity.

During the reception, a photo slide show displayed five years of images of Michael and me at church and community events.

The same month, I officiated a wedding in Dallas. I was marrying one of Harry Wooten's sons and his fiancée at Royal Lane. During the five years I'd lived in Oklahoma City, I had returned to Dallas almost monthly, maintaining my relationships with many people from Royal Lane, particularly the Wootens. Now I was about to move eleven hours away. The weekend of the wedding was like a last hurrah with the people who had been my friends when I took my first steps out of the closet.

In June, my sister Erin hosted a going-away dinner for the family at her house. We tried explaining where we were moving to my three-year-old nephew, who pronounced Nebraska "Numberaska." As Michael and I were leaving Erin's house after a rich evening together, she grabbed me in the tightest hug she'd given me in many years, and she began to cry.

"I'll miss you, brother," she said.

"I know," I responded. "I'll miss you too."

Then she said, "I love you."

Now I was crying as well. "I love you too."

As we drove off, Michael said, "I think everything has healed between you two."

"Feels that way." I stared out the passenger window, reflecting on the long journey of the last six years.

28

"What's so funny?"

"How's Omaha?" Pappoo asked. He had become a slight man, with thin, white hair. The red faux-leather sofa swallowed him. "Tell me about your church."

A few years before, he'd had pain in his groin and blood in his urine. At the time, Mom told the physician they didn't want to get five years down the road and learn that it was cancer.

"Let's figure it out now," she implored him. Well, almost five years down the road, after many hospitalizations, surgeries, and medications, we learned that the illness was indeed bladder cancer.

Pappoo was well into his eighties at this point, but he still wanted to fight the disease.

"Can't let us World War II guys disappear just yet," he told the doctor. I began to fear phone calls at odd times of the day, as they often reported a new ER visit or downturn in his condition. And every holiday became a potential last one.

"This could be Pappoo's last," became a regular refrain for most holidays. "Please come to Father's Day weekend, this could be Pappoo's last." When we arrived, we learned that he'd been rushed to the hospital that morning.

"Come to Thanksgiving, this could be Pappoo's last." So we changed our plans and drove instead to Miami. He looked frail. A month before, his local physician had said there was nothing more to be done. Mom had called a specialist in Joplin, Missouri, who told her to bring him immediately for emergency surgery.

That Thanksgiving we took one last, big, family photo, the only one with Michael in it. But Pappoo looks so frail and sick, I've never displayed our copy.

I made one last visit to Miami to see him in the spring of 2011.

He was interested in hearing about my ministry, so I told him how much I was enjoying the new church and answered all his questions. He asked about the building. Throughout my childhood he had been the chair of the Properties Committee of our church, so he always liked hearing about the various church buildings where I worked. Mom had already shown him photos of the large sanctuary with its mighty wooden rafters and beautiful stained glass windows. He was impressed, and proud that I was now serving such a large and prominent congregation.

We ate a sandwich, drank some Dr. Pepper, and watched a Western on TV. As usual, the volume was turned up loud. Without looking away from the show, he softly asked me, "How's Michael?"

"He's good. He wasn't able to come," I answered. "Thank you for asking."

When it was time to depart, I told him that I wasn't sure when I'd be back to visit. "The drive from Omaha is long, and I'm getting busier and busier at church and in the community."

"I understand," he said. "It's not a quick or easy trip."

He stood up carefully so that we could hug. "I love you, Scotty," he said.

"I love you, too."

He died in late June. I'd been about to leave for Tampa, Florida to attend the General Synod of the United Church of Christ. Mom's first call was from a hospital room to inform me that he was nearing the end. In the background, I could hear him wailing in pain. When Mom called again to tell us it was over, we were already packing. We arrived at Mom's house about midnight.

We were all up early the next morning. As Harold made coffee, Michael, Mom, and I sat out on the back deck enjoying a moment's rest, taking in the view of golden morning light reflecting across the surface of the water.

"I need your help today," Mom said.

"Whatever you need, Sandra," Michael answered.

"Yesterday I didn't get much help picking up and cleaning at Pappoo's house. We need to do that today, because tomorrow the family will all be there and lunch after the funeral will be at the house."

We drove to Miami after breakfast, wearing old clothes and armed with cleaning supplies and rags. My sister and Karen arrived as well, as did one cousin.

"You realize I'm the only in-law here?" Michael pointed out.

"Yeah, I do." I said sheepishly. "Thank you."

As we were carrying in supplies for cleaning and the food

and drinks for later, Mom called us over. "The most important thing I need you two to do is to get rid of the mattress."

"Okay," we said, somewhat puzzled. "What mattress?"

"The night before he died, your Uncle Frank found Pappoo in bed. He had bled all over. That's why the ambulance was called. I couldn't get the mattress out of the house by myself yesterday."

"What do you mean, by yourself?" I asked. "Weren't your brothers here?"

"Yes." Mom shook her head. "They refused to even enter the room."

Then she added, "Which means that the mattress has been in there for two days with the door closed. It's not going to be a pleasant task."

I rolled my eyes, wondering why my uncles hadn't taken care of the mattress the day before. Michael put a hand on my shoulder. "That's okay, Sandra. We'll take care of the mattress. What do we need to do?"

"I think you need to take the mattress and all the bedding to the city incinerator. The only vehicle that the mattress will fit in is the old truck."

I laughed, "That old thing? Does it still drive?" Pappoo had bought a brand-new truck in the early 1980s. Needless to say, by 2011 it wasn't in the greatest shape.

Mom answered, "The truck started the last time someone tried it. I'm not sure how long that's been. Why don't you go see if it will start?"

As we walked outside with the key, Michael said, "Your Mom doesn't need your attitude. I know you are annoyed at others for not helping and doing their part, but let's do this for her."

The gearshift was broken on the old truck. In its place were a pair of pliers. Fortunately, the transmission was automatic. The truck started, but only after a few tries and pumps on the gas pedal.

We turned the engine off and trusted it would start a second time. Then we went to the bedroom, where the smell was pretty strong. Mom, wearing bright yellow disposable plastic gloves, was removing the soiled bedsheets. "Here," she said, "I have gloves for you both." We put on our own bright yellow disposable plastic gloves, as we looked at the large bloodstain in the middle of the mattress.

"Let's get this mattress out of here," Mom said.

Michael and I lifted the blood-soaked mattress and carried it carefully through the house and out the door. As we hefted it into the back of the old truck, Pappoo's next door neighbor, my sister's fourth-grade teacher, walked across the street.

"Scotty, how's your grandpa?" she said.

"Mrs. Levo, he died yesterday," I answered.

"Oh," she said with surprise and concern. "I was worried when I saw all of your cars here today."

"Thank you," I responded, eager to get on with our unpleasant task.

"When is the funeral?" she asked, stepping closer.

"The visitation will be tonight at the funeral home. The service is tomorrow at ten at First Baptist."

She nodded. "Thank you. We'll be there." Then she added, "Oh, Scotty, he was such a kind man and a good neighbor."

"Thank you, Mrs. Levo." I smiled graciously.

"Is this your brother-in-law?" she asked, looking at Michael for the first time.

"No. This is my husband, Michael." I waited to see what came next, annoyed at having to come out in the midst of carrying my grandpa's deathbed to the garbage.

Michael took off a bright yellow disposable plastic glove and extended his hand to Mrs Levo. "Nice to meet you," he said.

"And you, too," she said, and shook his hand with kindness.

"Well, we have to get this mattress to the incinerator," I said, quite ready to complete our task.

"Oh." She looked at what we had been carrying, and the nature of our chore seemed to dawn on her. Backing away, she said, "I'll see you later, then."

It was midday at the beginning of July in northeastern Oklahoma, the hottest day of the year so far. As the truck engine turned over, Michael said, "It's got to be a hundred degrees. And even hotter in this truck. Does the AC work?"

I pushed the button. Nothing happened. So we rolled the windows all the way down.

We drove across town to the city incinerator. I showed the gate attendant Pappoo's water bill, which allowed us to dump for free. Workers guided me into the big bay.

I remembered the place from my adolescence, when I'd ride along with Dad when we had something to dump. The incinerator is a large metal building, kind of like an airplane hangar, with a wide sliding door allowing access. Inside, bulldozers were pushing the trash into towering piles that awaited their turn to be hoisted into the flames.

Large drops of sweat were rolling from our brows as we pulled in. "As if the day weren't hot enough," Michael said, looking at me with fake enthusiasm, "we're now inside a big metal building where there are fires burning." Then he added, "And I think the stench of the mattress is finally gone. It's being overpowered by the stench of the trash."

I chuckled at his wide, sarcastic grin.

We hopped out of the truck and yanked our bright yellow disposable plastic gloves back onto our hands. We opened the rear of the truck, pulled the mattress out, carried it a few feet, then tossed it onto one of the trash piles. We threw the bundle of sheets on top of the mattress. I peeled off my bright yellow disposable plastic gloves and threw them away as well.

"That's done," I declared. Then I wiped my brow on my sleeve, climbed in the driver's seat, and sighed deeply.

As we drove away from the incinerator, Michael started laughing.

"What's so funny?" I asked.

"The day is over 100 degrees. We are in this broken-down old truck. We don't have any air conditioning, and we just left the city dump where I helped to get rid of the bloody mattress of a man who didn't like me because I fell in love with his grandson."

I shook my head at the absurdity of it all, and Michael leaned back in his seat.

Hot air blew in through the open windows, drying some of our sweat.

AFTERWORD

If you are interested in resources related to LGBT-inclusive religion and spirituality, please check out Scott's website: www.escottjones.com